THE BACKGROUND
OF PASSION MUSIC

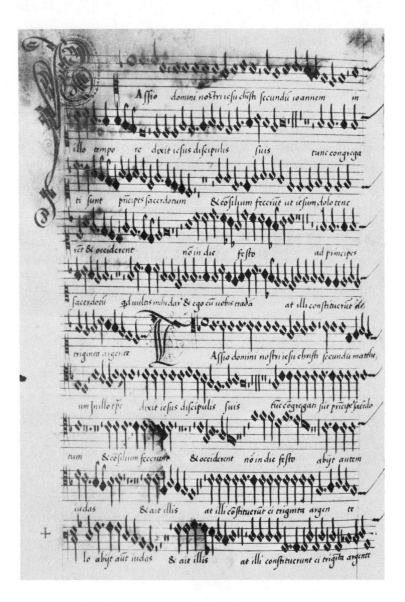

Exordium and opening section of the Longaval Passion (Biblioteca Nazionale Centrale, Florence, MS II.I.232, folios 130v and 131r; photos courtesy of the Bib. Naz. Cent.).

Assio domini nostri iesu christi secundum lucam in illo tempore   dixit iesus

discipulis suis Scitis quia post biduu pascha fiet & filius hominis tradetur

ut crucifigatur & seniores populi & consilium ut iesum dolo teneret & occideret

dicebant   autem   ne forte tumultus fieret in populo   ad princi

pes sacerdotum qd vultis mihi dar' & ego cum uob nada at illi cōstituerūt ei triginta

argenti   Verte   Assio domini nostri iesu christi secundū mar

cum in illo tempore   dixit iesus discipulis suis   Scitis qa post biduu

pascha fiet & filius hominis tradet' ut crucifigatur   principes sacerdotum

& seniores po puli   fecerunt ut iesu dolo tenerent & occi

derent dicebat autem   ne forte tumult' fieret   in popu

The Background
of Passion Music

J. S. Bach and his predecessors

BASIL SMALLMAN

Alsop Professor of Music
in the
University of Liverpool

SECOND REVISED AND ENLARGED EDITION

DOVER PUBLICATIONS, INC.

New York

Published in Canada by General Publishing Company, Ltd., 30 Lesmill Road, Don Mills, Toronto, Ontario.
Published in the United Kingdom by Constable and Company, Ltd., 10 Orange Street, London WC 2.

This Dover edition, first published in 1970, is a revised and enlarged republication of the work originally published by the SCM Press, Ltd., London, in 1957. The Preface to the Dover Edition, the Appendices and the Bibliography are entirely new features of the present edition.

International Standard Book Number: 0–486–22250–0
Library of Congress Catalog Card Number: 69–19465

Manufactured in the United States of America
Dover Publications, Inc.
180 Varick Street
New York, N. Y. 10014

PREFACE TO THE DOVER EDITION

THE publication of a new edition of this book has provided a welcome opportunity not only to correct some minor errors but also to incorporate a number of extensive additions to bring the information up to date. Alterations in the main body of the text have been limited to some very slight revisions, thus preserving the original character of the book, as a general survey with (it is hoped) a modest degree of readability. At the same time an entirely new section (ten Appendices in the form of extensive notes) has been added, to give more detailed information on a variety of important topics and to supply more thorough documentation; in order to preserve the historical sequence, and to enhance readability, the new appendices are placed in chronological order, rather than in the order of the references in the main text. Also the list of Passions available in modern editions has been considerably extended and a new Bibliography included, which should increase the value of the book as a work of reference. The final result is still, of course, not in any sense comprehensive; a detailed study of the whole subject in depth would involve several volumes of considerably larger size.

I should like to express my gratitude to Mr Alec Robertson for some very helpful criticism and advice, and also for his warm encouragement to me to expand the work to its new proportions.

BASIL SMALLMAN

The University of Liverpool
February 1970

PREFACE TO THE FIRST EDITION

T H E two great Passion compositions of J. S. Bach are widely recognized as being among the finest artistic achievements of European civilization. Over a period of many years, regular performances of these works at Passiontide have ensured their increasing acceptance as an essential part of the musical and religious life of most Christian communities. The aim of this short book is to examine these masterpieces in relation to their historical context and to show their position as the culmination of a musical and liturgical tradition of great antiquity. In tracing this historical background I have not attempted to produce a complete critical and analytical survey of early Passion music, but rather a broad study, couched in terms which should be clearly intelligible to the non-specialist reader, of the gradual growth of the musical language and of the religious philosophies which served Bach so supremely well for his personal expression of faith. It will be realized that this presentation of a comprehensive picture has necessarily entailed the sacrifice of a considerable amount of detail.

Bearing in mind the needs of the general reader I have adopted the policy throughout the book of providing straightforward definitions of the more difficult technical terms and expressions as they occur in the text; but any further assistance in this respect which may be necessary can be obtained from such a publication as the excellent Penguin *Dictionary of Music*, which gives clear and concise definitions of a wide range of musical terms.

It is also suggested that the reader will find it advantageous to have available for ready reference the vocal scores of the two Bach Passions. The best modern English editions, those by Sir Ivor Atkins (St John Passion), and Sir Edward Elgar and Sir Ivor Atkins (St Matthew Passion), both published by Novello and Co. Ltd, are the ones invariably used for quotation in this book.

I wish to express my sincere thanks to Professor the Reverend Canon Alan Richardson for his unfailing encouragement and advice, and to my colleagues Professor Ivor Keys and F. Metheringham Laming, both of whom read the book in typescript and made a number of valuable suggestions for its improvement. My thanks are also due to Miss Patience Robertson, who kindly allowed me to study her manuscript copy of the St Matthew Passion by Johann Meder.

BASIL SMALLMAN

The University,
Nottingham
May 1956

CONTENTS

I

INTRODUCTORY

IN the summer of 1722, the town council of Leipzig were
seeking to appoint a new Cantor for the ancient Lutheran
school of St Thomas, in succession to the famous composer
Johann Kuhnau who had died on June 5th after more than
twenty years' service. Leipzig, with its university, its Opera-
house and its great cosmopolitan fair was at this time rapidly
becoming one of the leading cultural centres in Germany, a
clearing-house for new ideas introduced by overland travellers,
just as Hamburg, the great North Sea port, was the principal
gateway by which new philosophies from overseas entered the
country. The town council, fully aware of their responsi-
bilities, were determined to find the best possible successor to
Kuhnau. Indeed for many of the councillors the death of
Kuhnau afforded an eagerly-awaited opportunity for bringing
the church music of the town into line with contemporary
taste; for adopting the melodious, theatrical style of composition which was rapidly gaining favour in other parts of
Germany. Kuhnau, a staunch advocate of tradition, had on
many past occasions expressed his displeasure at the increasing
popularity of operatic music in church, and under his influence
the musical parts of the services had retained a character
which by this time had become somewhat archaic. Now that
the opportunity for a change had occurred, it was clearly
desirable to attract to Leipzig a progressive young musician
who was well-versed in the latest musical techniques and
sufficiently renowned to be able to exercise a reforming
influence on the music of the town.

The position of Cantor at St Thomas's involved many important and varied duties. The tenets of orthodox Lutheranism
placed great emphasis on musical training as a subject for
serious study in the school, and in consequence the Cantor
occupied a high position in the hierarchy of teachers, being

inferior in rank only to the Rector and the sub-Rector. In addition to his duties as a music teacher, the Cantor was also expected to provide instruction to the lower forms of the school in Latin grammar and syntax and in the *Colloquia corderi* (a text-book of piety and etiquette), a requirement which proved a stumbling-block to many a celebrated musician.

Attached to the school was the great church of St Thomas, the principal church in Leipzig, which could boast an ancient musical tradition of a high standard of excellence. It was in the provision of music for the services of this church and at the sister establishment of St Nicholas that the major part of the Cantor's work lay. In the days of the great Cantors a Sunday would rarely pass when some new church composition of major proportions, a cantata, perhaps, or a motet, was not performed at one of the services. The burdens of such a position demanded an experienced musician of all-round musical and administrative ability and one who was a composer and performer of repute.

From a field of six distinguished candidates, the choice of the council immediately fell on G. P. Telemann (1681-1767), a composer who was renowned throughout Germany for his able championship of the elegant new operatic style in Protestant church music. Telemann was well-known in Leipzig as he had attended the university there in 1701, nominally as a student of law, and while at the university he had created a remarkable impression by his outstanding musical gifts, and had formed an important student music society which had later become a great power in the musical life of the town. In the course of an eventful career, he had scored considerable successes both with his work at the Opera-house and also with the church compositions which he was commissioned to write for regular performance at St Thomas's. Some years later he was appointed, without the consent of Kuhnau, to the post of organist at the so-called 'New' church in Leipzig, a medieval Franciscan foundation which had been restored to use at the end of the seventeenth century after a long period of neglect since early Reformation times, but he soon relinquished this position in favour of a better one as Capellmeister at Sorau. Since the end of 1721 he had held office as director of the Opera theatre in Hamburg where, with an almost ceaseless flow of new compositions, he had achieved great fame. In response to the invitation of the Leipzig council, Telemann, despite an understandable reluctance to undertake the non-musical teaching, at first accepted the vacant post of Cantor. But some time later, after receiving a salary increase of a few hundred thalers at Hamburg, he wrote somewhat ungraciously to withdraw his acceptance.

The second choice of the council was Christoph Graupner (1683-1760), a musician of high repute, who held the position of Capellmeister at Darmstadt. Like Telemann, Graupner had strong connections with Leipzig as he had studied under Kuhnau for nine years at the school of St Thomas, where he had distinguished himself in clavier playing and composition. In his turn Graupner expressed willingness to accept the vacant Cantorate, but he too was later forced to withdraw his candidature as he was unable to secure release from his employment with the Landgrave of Hesse-Darmstadt.

In these provoking circumstances, the Leipzig council decided that (in the words of one of its members) 'since the best man could not be obtained, mediocre ones would have to be accepted.' And so, from the remaining field of 'mediocre' musicians, their choice finally fell on Johann Sebastian Bach, a late and somewhat hesitant applicant for the post.

Since 1717 Bach had held office as Capellmeister to the youthful Prince Leopold of Anhalt-Cöthen, who was a cultivated amateur musician and a liberal and kindly patron. This had been a period of great comfort and prosperity for the composer, despite the deep personal loss which he had suffered in 1720 by the death of his first wife, Maria Barbara, a tragedy which had been considerably mitigated by his happy choice of Anna Magdalena Wülcken as her successor just over a year later. Encouraged by the enthusiastic support of his young patron, Bach had been able to develop his creative gifts in an atmosphere of peace and security and had rapidly gained an enviable reputation throughout Lutheran Germany as an outstanding performer on the organ and harpsichord and as a composer of great profundity and scholarship. Without doubt, his reputation was as high at Leipzig as it was elsewhere; the derogatory opinion of the town councillor, quoted above, is simply an indication that he was not regarded as the ideal person for the task of modernizing Leipzig's church music. Bach's sympathies were known to lie with the ancient Lutheran church traditions and against the elegant Italianate style which was so rapidly gaining in popularity. The very features of style and emotional expression in Bach's music which later generations have so much admired were regarded by his more advanced contemporaries as an anachronistic adherence to an outworn musical language, if not as sheer pedantry.

Bach's reasons for wishing to leave his congenial employment at Cöthen are worth examination. The external event which provided an immediate stimulus was the marriage contracted in 1721 between Prince Leopold and the Princess Frederike Henrietta of Anhalt-Bernburg. The Princess had no love for music and would tolerate no such powerful rival in the affections of her young husband. Under her influence, the Prince began to show an increasingly cool attitude towards the art which he had formerly championed so whole-heartedly. This partial withdrawal of patronage must have warned Bach that the time had come for him to seek his fortune elsewhere. Furthermore, it must have been clear to Bach that a large town like Leipzig, with its university and its famous Lutheran schools, would offer far greater educational scope to his growing family than could possibly be found in a sheltered retreat like Cöthen.

But even more important, probably, than such material considerations, must have been Bach's realization that one side of his creative nature could never find full expression in his existing mode of life. At Cöthen, the asceticism of the Reformed (Calvinist) church services, the tiny organs and the small and inefficient choirs afforded little opportunity for the development of artistic church music. During his tenure of office there, Bach was cut off almost entirely from this type of composition, which had formed an important part of his work during his earlier life at Arnstadt, Mühlhausen, and Weimar, and he devoted himself mainly to the cultivation of orchestral and instrumental chamber music. To this period belong the Brandenburg and the various solo concertos, the numerous sonatas and suites for stringed and keyboard instruments and the first book of the *Forty-eight Preludes and Fugues*. By accepting the vacant Cantorate at Leipzig, he would again have the important duties of a church composer to undertake, and would find excellent resources for the development of his natural affinities for sacred music.

Faced by so many conflicting considerations and not

uninfluenced by a personal reluctance to exchange his exalted social position as a Capellmeister to a royal court for the relatively humble one of town Cantor, Bach delayed his application for the vacant post until late in the year 1722. But once his final decision had been taken he set out, with characteristic energy and determination, to prepare himself fully for his new duties. After the withdrawal of Christoph Graupner in January 1723, Bach's appointment seemed assured and, if events took a normal course, the formal installation ceremony would take place in April in time for the new Cantor to officiate in church during the celebration of Holy Week. During the intervening period, therefore, Bach concentrated mainly on the composition of a large-scale setting of the Passion story with which he expected to make his first important appearance before the Leipzig public. As it turned out, Bach's installation as Cantor was delayed until the beginning of June 1723, but there are grounds for believing that this newly-composed Passion was performed as planned in St Thomas's on Good Friday of that year, while Bach was still a candidate for the post, though this is by no means proved.[1]

Passion music was for Bach a new and untried field of composition; in this earliest attempt, a setting of St John's account, there are, as we shall see later, many indications of the difficulty which the composer found in the compilation of his text. Owing to the lack of a suitable literary collaborator and to the considerable pressure on his time, Bach was forced to gather his lyrical (non-Gospel) text from a number of different sources with a resultant lack of artistic unity in the work as a whole. In his later settings of the Passion, of which there were certainly two, and possibly three, Bach enlisted the help of the Leipzig poet, C. F. Henrici (1700-1764), who wrote under the pseudonym, Picander.

Picander's first Passion libretto, dating from 1725, is typical of the religious texts of the period in its abandonment of the Gospel narrative, its obvious insincerity, and its frequent lapses of taste. A characteristic example occurs in the account of the procession to Calvary, in which the women following the Saviour are described as proceeding 'not on foot, but swimming in the torrents of their tears'. It is possible that Bach set this libretto to music, though it is hard to believe

[1] See C. S. Terry, *Bach: the Passions*, Bk 1, Oxford University Press, 1928, pp. 11-12.

that the poem would have satisfied him; but the score, if it ever existed, has not survived.

At a later stage in their collaboration Bach was able to exercise a considerably greater influence over Picander, an influence which is easily discernible in the text of the great St Matthew Passion (1729), in which the exact Gospel words are retained for the narrative portions and far greater use is made of the traditional hymn verses, which are selected and placed with obvious care, probably by Bach himself. Picander's share in the text was confined to the provision of suitable lyrical material for the many reflective arias, duets, and choruses, a function which he fulfilled with considerable skill.

In 1731 Picander wrote a further Passion text based on St Mark's account, and this is definitely known to have been set to music by Bach. The score of the work has long since disappeared, but the music of some of the lyrical portions has survived in the *Trauer-Ode* which Bach composed in 1727 for the funeral of Queen Christiane Eberhardine, a staunch Protestant who had achieved fame by preferring the abandonment of her rights as the Queen of Poland to the renunciation of her religious beliefs. This adaptation of the music of the *Trauer-Ode* for use in the St Mark Passion is but one example of Bach's frequent custom of 'borrowing' the music of an earlier composition for a new work which was urgently needed. A parallel instance is provided by the Funeral music which Bach produced in 1728 for the obsequies of his former patron Prince Leopold of Anhalt-Cöthen. At this time, Bach was busily engaged on the St Matthew Passion and, as he had insufficient leisure to compose an original work for the Prince's funeral, he invited Picander to fit suitable words to some of the movements from the Passion which were already complete. In this case, the Passion has of course survived, while the score of the Funeral music is lost. (see App. IX, p. 155)

Thus, in all, Bach is known to have composed three or, if the Picander Passion of 1725 is included, four Passions.[1] Of these only two, the St John (1723) and the St Matthew (1729) have survived complete.

[1] There also exists a St Luke Passion, the score of which is partly in Bach's handwriting. The work is almost certainly not authentic, as the music is unlike Bach's at any period of his life. Bach is known to have been an assiduous student of other men's music, and this manuscript is very probably a fair copy of a Passion by an earlier north-German composer.

No more difficult type of composition could have fallen to the lot of the composer at the outset of his career in Leipzig. Such were the problems which surrounded Passion composition that affront would inevitably be given to one or other of the religious sects in the town. To gain a fuller understanding of these problems we must first consider some of the religious dissensions which had troubled Germany during the previous fifty years.

In the course of the seventeenth century, orthodox Lutheranism had become, in opposition to the tenets of Luther himself, highly intellectualized and dogma-ridden. The reformer's original doctrines of simple, heart-felt faith, strict adherence to the message of the Bible, and recognition of the universal priesthood of all believers, were being overridden by a new priestly caste who claimed the exclusive right to interpret God's word in the light of their own abstruse theological scholarship. By comparison with the lifeless formalism which arose from such teaching, the Calvinist branch of the Reformed Church showed remarkable humanism in the emphasis which it laid on practical Christianity, on the expression of faith by good works, rather than by the strict observance of doctrinal minutiae.

The first signs of a reaction against orthodox Lutheranism appeared in the last quarter of the seventeenth century under the leadership of Jacob Spener (1635-1705) who, after completing his theological studies at Strasbourg, had spent a year in Geneva where he had been much impressed by the simplicity and sincerity of Calvinist ecclesiastical discipline. In 1675 Spener published his celebrated Reform document entitled *Pia desideria*, which contained six main proposals for the guidance of his followers. These proposals were, (i) that the Bible should be studied in private meetings among Christians, (ii) that the laity should regain their position as a common priesthood and their rights to share in the spiritual government of the church, (iii) that a new emphasis should be placed on practical Christianity, (iv) that unbelievers should be approached with greater sympathy and understanding, (v) that increased value should be attached to the cultivation of the ' devotional life' in theological training, and (vi) that a more direct and emotional type of preaching should be encouraged.

This new evangelical movement called, half in mockery,

Pietism, gained a large following amongst both the priesthood and the laity and its teaching spread rapidly over central and northern Germany. Pietism was introduced into Leipzig by the preacher Hermann Francke, who gained considerable popularity amongst the townsfolk. Owing, however, to the powerful opposition of the many orthodox theologians in Leipzig, Francke and his followers were forced to leave the town and they removed to Halle where they founded an important new university. After the death of Spener in 1705 Francke assumed the leadership of the Pietist movement and Halle became the leading centre of the new sect.

Pietism constituted a grave menace to Lutheran church music. Following to some extent the austere example of the Calvinist Church, the Pietists discountenanced the use of all music in the services except simple hymns and pious songs of an emotional and frequently sentimental nature, a limitation which afforded little scope to church musicians for the development of their art. Bach himself had suffered from the influence of Pietism during an early period of his career. While organist at St Blasius's, Mühlhausen, between 1707 and 1708, the composer came into frequent conflict with the Superintendent of the church, J. A. Frohne, who had strong Pietist leanings.

The poetic revolt against these new doctrines came principally from Erdmann Neumeister, a pastor of St Jacob's, Hamburg, who, recognizing the shallowness of this new cult of simplicity and sentimentality and fearing for its effect upon the development of church art, produced, in 1700, a cycle of cantata texts which were based on the form of the operatic libretto and thus afforded composers greatly enriched opportunities for musical elaboration. These cantata texts, and the many imitations which soon followed, scored a considerable success with the Hamburg public; and, despite a few scandalized protests, the majority of orthodox Lutherans, recognizing the effectiveness of this new weapon in the fight against Pietism, warmly approved the new poetic and musical artforms which were created. Nevertheless the influence of Pietist poetry is plainly discernible in many of these sacred libretti, in the emotionalism and the highly-coloured religiosity which characterizes much of the verse. The Picander Passion libretto of 1725, mentioned above, is a typical example.

The introduction of the new operatic style of composition into the Passion genre gave rise, as we shall see later, to the 'Opera' Passions which were produced in Hamburg in the early eighteenth century. As may be imagined, such productions aroused intense hostility among the Pietists. But it is important to realize that many orthodox musicians and theologians also, who had no inclination towards Pietism, but who revered the traditional music of the Lutheran Church, could feel little sympathy with this revolutionary new style of church composition. As we have seen earlier, Kuhnau, the late Cantor of St Thomas's, was just such a traditionalist.

At Leipzig, the traditional type of Passion setting, in which the narrative and the utterances by individual characters were delivered in unaccompanied plainsong and the crowd sayings by a choir singing simple chordal responses, had been presented without interruption for nearly two centuries until 1721, when Kuhnau, yielding to the pressure of contemporary opinion, had produced an Oratorio version of St Mark's account. The Oratorio type of Passion which derived many features, such as the recitative and aria and the use of accompanying instruments, from the seventeenth-century Italian Oratorio, was hardly a novelty in 1721. During the course of the previous century the new form had been adopted by many German composers, mainly in the progressive cultural centres on the northern seacoast, such as Hamburg, Danzig and Königsberg. Further inland, at large towns like Dresden and Leipzig, a more conservative outlook prevailed and the influence of the new musical styles was less readily admitted to church composition. Kuhnau's St Mark Passion of 1721 was probably written partly as a sop for the Leipzig intelligentsia and partly as an attempt to show a *via media* between the simplicity of the traditional settings and the lurid excesses of the Hamburg Opera style. But doubtless even this well-mannered breach with tradition aroused considerable opposition from the conservative and Pietist elements in Leipzig.

It is probably a mistake to regard the Leipzig council as being unanimous in their desire for a really advanced 'reform' Cantor to succeed Kuhnau. We find, for example, from records of the election proceedings which led to the appointment of Bach, that the Dominus consul, Dr Steger, while voting for Bach, expressed the desire that 'he would make compositions that were not theatrical'. And further we learn, from one of the conditions of appointment, that 'in order to preserve the good order in the churches', Bach is expected 'so to arrange the music that it shall not last too long, and shall be of such a nature as not to make an operatic impression, but rather to incite the listeners to devotion'. Such indications of timidity on the part of the Leipzig council were very probably prompted by recollections of the public scandals which had followed some of the sacred operatic performances in Hamburg at the beginning of the century.

Very few people in the early eighteenth century can have recognized the sublimity of Bach's great Passion settings. The citizens of Leipzig, in particular, whether of conservative or progressive inclinations, must have been singularly unprepared for so great an advance in musical and religious thought. An interesting and amusing picture of conservative reaction to the modern style occurs in a book by Christian Gerber entitled *The History of Church Ceremonies in Saxony*. This was published in 1732, three years after the first performance of Bach's St Matthew Passion, which may in fact be the work referred to in the following passage: 'Fifty and more years ago it was the custom for the organ to remain silent in church on Palm Sunday, and on that day, because it was the beginning of Holy Week, there was no music. But gradually the Passion story, which had formerly been sung in simple plainchant, humbly and reverently, began to be sung with many kinds of instruments in the most elaborate fashion, occasionally mixing in a little setting of a Passion Chorale which the whole congregation joined in singing, and then the mass of instruments fell to again. When in a large town this Passion music was done for the first time, with 12 violins (strings), many oboes, bassoons, and other instruments, many people were astonished and did not know what to make of it. In the pew of a noble family in church, many Ministers and Noble Ladies were present, who sang the first Passion Chorale out of their books with great devotion. But when this theatrical music began, all these people were thrown into the greatest bewilderment, looked at each other, and said: "What will come of this?" An old widow of the nobility said: "God save us, my children! It's just as if one were at an Opera Comedy." But everyone was genuinely displeased by it and voiced many just complaints against it. There are, it is true, some people who take pleasure in such idle things, especially if they are of sanguine temperament and inclined to sensual pleasure. Such persons defend large-scale church compositions as best they may, and hold others to be crotchety and of melancholy temperament—as if they alone possessed the wisdom of Solomon, and others had no understanding.'[1]

The more progressive elements at Leipzig were probably equally unresponsive to Bach's masterpieces. Bach belonged spiritually and technically to an artistic epoch which was rapidly becoming outmoded. At once the most original and eclectic of composers, he was destined to gather together the threads of the past and to infuse new life and expression into the musical language and forms of his predecessors. By the second half of his life, the elaborate, architectural musical art which had been developed in Germany by generations of Protestant musicians was rapidly giving place to the elegant, melodious music of the approaching age of Reason. Bach's own sons were reaching maturity in an age whose artistic ideals were far removed from those of their father. 'Music,' said Carl Philipp Emmanuel, his second son, in a slighting reference to the complexity of Baroque art, 'need not be a great party where all the people speak simultaneously.'

The rapidly changing styles and tastes of this period account very largely for the neglect of Bach's music for well over half a century after his death. Bach's masterpieces suffered a common neglect with all the art of his epoch, much of it admittedly worthless, until 1829, when Mendelssohn rediscovered the St Matthew Passion and performed the work in Berlin, exactly one hundred years after its first performance, thereby re-awakening the world to a new awareness of Bach's greatness and stimulating an interest in his music which has increased steadily ever since.

In this short study an attempt will be made to relate Bach's Passion music to its historical background and in particular to the important developments which occurred gradually during the seventeenth century, when many new features which were later to be idealized in Bach's settings made their first appearance. For this purpose it has seemed most appropriate to divide the study of the works according to the musical techniques and forms employed, rather than into a simple historical sequence, and by means of such a division to isolate

[1] H. T. David and A. Mendel, *The Bach Reader*, W. W. Norton and Co., New York, 1945, pp. 229-230.

the various dramatic and lyrical elements used in the unfolding of the story. Thus a consideration of the development of the technique of recitative will involve an examination of the dramatic functions of the Evangelist and of the various individual characters, while a study of the use of the chorale and the solo aria will necessarily reveal the part played by lyrical commentary in the presentation of the drama. In this way, an investigation of the Passion compositions of earlier composers will be found to give a remarkable insight into Bach's own aims and into the significance of many important features of his work.

As a first step in this task, we must turn back to the earliest Christian times to find the origins of Passion composition and then proceed to review briefly the historical development of the form during the medieval and renaissance periods.

II

THE MEDIEVAL AND
RENAISSANCE BACKGROUND

In the early Christian Church, the events of Passiontide were commemorated in two distinct ways, one primarily dramatic and the other primarily musical, both of which had their origins in the sacred liturgy.

The dramatic presentation of the story took the form of Passion plays which, together with similar celebrations for the Nativity and the Resurrection, are known to have been presented in church during the Middle Ages with considerable elaboration and theatrical effect, including costumes, music and stage properties. These liturgical dramas, which were regarded as an important medium of popular religious education, evolved gradually from the custom of introducing sung dialogues into the church services on the principal feast days, a custom which, in its turn, had originated in the *Tropes*—the interpolated phrases or verses which were used to ornament the music of the Mass. A well-known example of such a sacred dialogue is the *Quem quaeritis* which was designed for Eastertide performance and briefly outlines the story of the Resurrection. In this scene, an angel is shown seated beside a veil which represents the winding-sheet in Christ's tomb; the three Marys approach seeking the Saviour's body, and in the course of a short, sung dialogue, the angel lifts the veil to reveal the empty tomb and announces the triumphant news of Christ's Resurrection.

Originally these simple scenes were presented in the Latin tongue, were sung to a form of Gregorian plainchant and were acted solemnly and reverently before the altar by the clergy. But later, as growing secularization by lay actors led to the use of the vernacular and to a considerable increase in dramatic realism, such performances were transferred to the nave or to the porch of the church. In the Middle Ages, a church was regarded not solely as a place of public worship but also as a central unifying force in the community, as a common meeting-place, as a refuge from spiritual and material ills, and often as a grand patron of the arts. The use of the church by laymen for theatrical purposes, such as the mystery or miracle plays, naturally only strengthened its position as a guide and guardian in the lives of the people and in no way detracted from its purely sacred liturgical functions. There are few surviving examples of the early Passion plays, but their more modern descendants are easily recognizable in the religious theatrical performances which are still regularly given at Oberammergau, and at Thiersee in the Austrian Tyrol.

The purely musical presentation of the Passion is even more ancient in origin and even more firmly rooted in the liturgy. At least as early as the fifth century, the liturgy for Holy Week included plainchant settings of the four Gospel accounts of the Passion which appeared within the framework of the Mass in place of the normal Gospel reading. By tradition, St Matthew's version was given on Palm Sunday, St Mark's and St Luke's on Tuesday and Wednesday in Holy Week, and St John's on Good Friday. Originally the complete presentation of the Passion was the task of a single deacon, who distinguished between the narrative portions, the sayings of Christ, and the utterances of the *synagoga* (which included all the minor characters and the crowd or *Turba*), simply by altering the pitch and inflection of his voice; the Evangelist's part lay in the tenor range, that of Christ in the bass, and that of the *synagoga* in the alto. (See Appendix I, p. 123)

The use of Passion tones, as the simple plainsong formulas are known, admitted little scope for characterization, though medieval church rubrics have survived which indicate that the various 'voice-parts' were presented with some degree of realism. Durandus, the great French church authority, who died in 1296, directs in his *Rationale Divinorum Officiorum* that the words of Christ should be sung with sweetness, those of the Evangelist in the formal Gospel tone, and those of the 'most impious Jews' in a loud and harsh manner.[1] This type of impersonation, which appears to be a formidable task for a single cleric, is paralleled by the directions which appear in

[1] '. . . *Verba vero impiissimorum Judaeorum clamose et cum asperitate vocantur.*'

22

some of the manuscripts of the ancient liturgical plays, demanding an actor with a soft voice for the part of Jesus and one with a sharp and unpleasant voice for the rôle of Judas. From the fifteenth century, a dialogue form was adopted for the presentation of the Passion in which the separate vocal parts were entrusted to three clergy, a priest for the part of Christ, a deacon for the narrator, and a sub-deacon for the *synagoga*, thereby making possible an increased range of vocal expression and greater dramatic realism. A definitive version of the Passion tones was published in Rome in 1586 by a musician named Guidetti, working under the direction of Pope Sixtus the fifth, and this mode of Passion performance has survived practically unaltered to the present day.

The earliest known attempts at a more elaborate type of Passion composition were made in the middle of the fifteenth century by an unknown English composer. In these settings,[1] which are of St Matthew and St Luke, the traditional plain-song of the *synagoga* part is abandoned in favour of a freely-composed polyphonic version for three voice-parts. The rôles of Christ and the Evangelist were presumably intended to be sung to a form of plainsong, though its exact nature is not known, as the traditional Passion tones will not link up musically with the choral *synagoga* part.[2] These early English Passions are a comparatively recent discovery and it would be unwise to assume that they were the first of their kind or even that this type of Passion composition, the so-called Dramatic Passion, was of English origin. It seems quite possible that these two settings were composed in a traditional manner which was already well-established and that they may even have been based on earlier continental models which have not survived. Two further anonymous Passions have survived which are almost certainly of Italian origin, but these were composed rather later than the English specimens mentioned above, probably c. 1490.[3] The earliest Passion composer who has been definitely identified is the Englishman, Richard Davy, whose work (a setting of St Matthew) also dates from the last

---

[1] Source: British Museum. Egerton MS. 3307.
[2] See M. Bukofzer, *Studies in Medieval and Renaissance Music*, N.Y., 1950, p. 113 et seq.
[3] Source: Modena Estense. MS. Lat. 455 (M.1.12.). See also M. Bukofzer, op. cit., pp. 184-5.

decade of the fifteenth century. In this setting, the choral versions of the crowd utterances are grafted on to the traditional plainsong Passion tones which are used for the rôles of the Evangelist and of Christ. This became the established custom which was followed by numerous Passion composers during the sixteenth century. (See App. II, p. 124)

From a host of composers of many nationalities who cultivated the Dramatic Passion form during the sixteenth century, a few important names emerge, notably the Netherlander, Lassus; the Spaniard, Victoria; and the Englishman, William Byrd. Latin was of course the official language used by all the composers who were writing for the Roman ritual, regardless of their nationality; as we shall see later, when we come to consider in more detail the development of the crowd chorus, these Latin settings were stereotyped in form and conceived in a manner which was ritualistic rather than realistic.

In Germany, a number of Lutheran composers also adopted the new Passion form, but based their settings on a German version of the various Gospel accounts taken from Luther's own translation of the Bible. It is difficult to exaggerate the vividness of the impact on every branch of contemporary life in Germany which must have resulted from the dissemination at this time of religious, philosophical and scientific thought in the living tongue of the people. For many educated men a whole new world of ideas, which had formerly been the exclusive province of the Latin scholar, now became readily accessible. In the religious sphere particularly it made possible a new popular approach to the teachings of the Bible and to the understanding of church doctrines. Thus, despite their obvious similarities of musical form and structure, these German Dramatic Passions are fundamentally different in conception from their Latin counterparts. In the work of Johann Walter, Luther's principal musical adviser, who produced the first German settings (c. 1550), every effort is made to present the text with the utmost clarity. The composer deliberately sets aside all elaborate artistic devices in favour of a simple type of choral declamation which reproduces the natural rhythms of speech, and thus presents the story clearly and realistically. In this simple style, we can detect a reaction against the use of *melisma* (the setting of many notes to one word or syllable), which characterizes much of the Catholic church music of this period and even appears to a limited extent in the crowd choruses of the Latin Passions. Such *melismatic* treatment, while capable of producing many expressive musical effects, naturally obscures the clarity of the words and reduces the force of their dramatic impact considerably.

In the ancient plainsong Passions, after the scene of the death of Jesus, there occurs the rubric '*Hic genuflectitur et pausatim aliquantulum*', indicating a pause for silent meditation by the worshippers. This idea was adopted by Walter in his St Matthew Passion where, at the same place in the narrative, a pause is marked to permit silent prayer, '*Unser Vater*' (Our Father); the specification of a vernacular prayer at this point is an indication of the growing importance attached to congregational understanding and participation.

About ten years after these Passions by Johann Walter, there appeared an unusual German setting of St John's account by Antonio Scandello, an Italian composer who spent the greater part of his life in Germany. In this work, which later attained great popularity, an attempt is made to achieve a more artistic musical effect by confining the use of plainsong to the narration of the Evangelist and by setting the words of the various living characters, including Jesus, for a choir with a varying number of voice-parts; Pilate and Jesus for example are represented by a choir of three and four voice-parts respectively. This abandonment of realism in favour of greater artistry is symptomatic of the lack of dramatic resource inherent in the musical techniques of this period. In the typical Dramatic Passion form, the terse crowd utterances, which had to be set very simply in order to achieve any vividness of effect, provided composers with little scope for the exercise of their powers of artistic musical composition. Only in the opening and final choruses (the *Introitus* and *Gratiarum Actio*) were there opportunities for the use of a slightly more elaborate musical technique. It is not surprising therefore to find that a further type of Passion was developed during the sixteenth century which was based on the form of the motet. (See Appendix III, p. 131)

In the Motet Passion the complete text is sung throughout by an unaccompanied choir; solo voices are not used, but a limited degree of characterization is often achieved by allotting the spoken words of the individual characters to a reduced number of voices (usually two), in contrast with the

25

full four- or five-part choir who sing the words of narration and the utterances of the crowd. As a method of presenting the Passion story this form clearly lacks vividness and realism, but it compensates for this by providing a highly sensitive medium for emotional musical expression. Usually a link was retained with the older plainsong type of Passion by the use of the Passion tones, woven into the choral texture and placed in the appropriate voice-part: in the bass for Jesus, in the tenor for the Evangelist, and in the alto for the *synagoga*.

At the beginning of the sixteenth century, there appeared a Latin setting of the Passion according to St Matthew in the form of an extended motet divided into three sections (or *partes*). Until fairly recently, this setting was thought to be the work of the famous Netherlander, Jacobus Obrecht, but the discovery of some early manuscripts has now shown conclusively that Antoine de Longueval (or Longaval) was the composer.[1] The text is unusual; by a skilful combination of salient features from all four Gospels, a single composite account is produced which avoids the special characteristics of any particular Gospel. The three separate *partes* present in turn (i) the betrayal of Jesus and His arraignment before Caiaphas, (ii) the trial before Pilate, and (iii) the Crucifixion. The third section is devoted entirely to a complete recital of the 'Seven last Words from the Cross', taken from their various contexts in the four Gospels, and the whole work ends with a *Gratiarum actio*, 'qui passus est pro nobis, miserere nobis'. In his setting of the opening *Introitus*, the composer pays due regard to the impartiality shown by the unknown compiler of the text; the four-part chorus together sing the words '*Passio Domini nostri Jesu Christi secundum . . .*' (The Passion of our Lord Jesus Christ according to . . .), and at this point each voice announces the name of a different Evangelist; the soprano sings '*Johannem*', the alto '*Lucam*', the tenor '*Matthaeum*', and the bass '*Marcum*'.

During the sixteenth century, many Passions in this motet style were composed to both Latin and German texts. The majority of Roman Catholic composers adopted the Longaval text, though there are some interesting exceptions to this rule

[1] See A. Smijers, *De Matthaeus-Passie van Jacob Obrecht*, Tijdschrift der Vereeniging voor Nederlandsche Muziekgeschiedenis, XIV (1935), p. 182. (See Appendix IV, p. 136)

as, for example, the St John Passion (c. 1543) by Balthazar Harzer (usually known as Resinarius). Resinarius, who in later life became bishop of the diocese of Leipa in Bohemia, sets a Latin text which is divided into five *partes* and which, curiously enough, is clearly intended for Protestant use. A setting of a similar text was made in 1578 by Ludovicus Daser, Lassus's predecessor as Capellmeister to the court at Munich, and this provides a further example of a Latin setting which was intended for use in the Reformed liturgy. It is a mistake to imagine that in the early days of the Reformation there was an immediate and complete change-over to the liturgical use of the German language or indeed that Luther himself necessarily desired such a change. In his preface to the *Deutsche Messe* (1526) the Reformer even makes the suggestion (while admitting its impossibility in practice) 'that we sing and read from the Scriptures in all four languages, one Sunday in German, the next in Latin, the third in Greek, the fourth in Hebrew'. Certainly Luther encouraged co-operation between musicians of both churches and he himself sought the advice of the Catholic composer, Ludwig Senfl, on various matters connected with the formation of the new liturgy.

The first Motet Passion using a German text was composed in 1568 by the Magdeburg composer Joachim à Burck. Like the Longaval Passion, this work is divided into three *partes* but makes use of the text of St John's Gospel only. Thus, in the final section, instead of a complete recital of the Seven Last Words, only those three which properly belong to St John's account are included. Burck's text became the standard one for all later German settings of St John, with the exception of a most interesting and beautiful work by Leonhard Lechner, perhaps the finest of all the surviving Motet Passions. Lechner, who was born in the Tyrol, was brought up as a Catholic, but later turned Protestant. He studied under Lassus at Munich and eventually became Capellmeister at Stuttgart where he died in 1606. Possibly because of his early Catholic training, Lechner displays in his St John Passion (1594) many features of the early Catholic type of Motet Passion, including the presentation of all the Seven Last Words in the final section and the use of the Passion tones woven into the texture. His division of the text into five *partes* suggests however that his model may have been the Resinarius Passion.

The inherent lack of dramatic realism in the Motet Passion

caused a rapid decay of the form in the early seventeenth century. The last known example is a remarkable German setting of St John's account by Christoph Demantius which dates from 1631. In this work, a rich six-part setting, the expressive new harmonic techniques of the period are applied to the ancient form in a most striking way, a notable feature being the use of the musical *sharp* sign to symbolize the sharpness of the Crucifixion nails.[1] The decay of the Motet Passion was of course an inevitable consequence of the fundamental change in the whole development of music which began during the final years of the sixteenth century. Radical changes in musical forms and textures at this time brought about a decline in the vocal polyphonic style, which had culminated in the work of Palestrina, Lassus, Victoria and Byrd, and initiated a fresh exploration of the dramatic and emotional powers of the art. The traditional Dramatic type of Passion on the other hand, which fulfilled in a simple way a necessary liturgical function, and which was less consciously conceived as a work of art, continued an independent existence until a much later period.

It was at Florence, in Italy, at the turn of the century, that expression was first given to the revolutionary new ideas which were to change the course of musical history. A small group of intellectuals—poets, philosophers, musicians—believing themselves to be inspired by the ideals of classical Greece, advocated a new relationship between poetry and music, in which music was to serve a subordinate purpose as a vehicle for the dramatic and emotional presentation of verse. In place of the rich interweaving of voices, typical of renaissance polyphony, which they regarded as detrimental to poetry, the Florentine innovators wished to substitute the voice of a solo singer supported only by chords on an accompanying instrument, and in this way to achieve a realistic form of musical rhetoric. In his preface to the *Nuove Musiche*, a collection of arias and madrigals in the new style, Caccini, one of the leading musicians of the Florentine group, summarizes these artistic aims in the words ' I conceived the idea of composing a harmonic speech, a sort of music in which a noble restraint was placed on the singing in favour of the words.'

The practical application of these theories resulted in the creation of a new form, Opera, a tentative experiment at first, but soon to be raised by the genius of Claudio Monteverdi

[1] See Appendix V, p. 140.

(1567-1643) to the status of a major art-form. In the wake of Opera, as its sacred counterpart, there followed the development of Oratorio, in which the 'pious affections' were found to be equally susceptible to the emotionalism of the new style. Opera and Oratorio developed along very similar lines, using identical musical techniques but differing in subject matter and in methods of dramatic presentation. For their libretti, the early Italian Opera composers turned to the myths of classical antiquity, such as Orpheus and Eurydice, Daphne, and Ariadne; while the Oratorio composers of the same period found inspiration in such Old Testament stories as Jephtha, Daniel, and Jonah. In Opera, the drama was presented directly on the stage as a play with sung dialogue, whereas in Oratorio direct stage action was avoided by the use of the *Historicus*, a narrator who linked the scenes together with descriptive narrative and introduced the words of the various characters, a function which is obviously paralleled by that of the Evangelist in the ancient Dramatic Passion. From Caccini's 'harmonic speech', there evolved the *recitative*, an essential feature of musical drama which will be examined in greater detail in a later chapter, and the *aria*, a highly-organized melodic type of vocal solo in which the claims of poetry are once again subordinated to those of music—and frequently the claims of both to the vanity of the solo singer! Experiments in Venice in the late sixteenth century by the famous *Maestro di Cappella* at St Mark's, Giovanni Gabrieli (1557-1612), led to the use of mixed groups of wind and stringed instruments, both independently and in combination with voices—the *concertato* style of composition. Such orchestras were not at first fully standardized but soon the stringed instruments, viols and violins, came to be recognized as an excellent medium for choral accompaniment and as an essential foundation for the contrasting tone-colours of the wind instruments.

One constant feature which characterizes all the music of this period is the presence of the *basso continuo*. This was a system of musical shorthand in which the given bass part was marked with figures placed beneath it (the so-called 'figured bass'). These figures indicated the essential harmonies which had to be played by the performer, while the details of note-spacing and part progression were left to his powers of extemporization. The principal *continuo* player performed, naturally, on an instrument capable of playing chords, such as the organ, harpsichord, lute, or guitar, while one or more of the bass instruments of the orchestra would be entrusted with the task of sustaining the bass line. As a natural result of the use of this system, the outer parts of a musical composition received a new emphasis. In contrast to the elaborate polyphonic music of the renaissance period in which every thread in the texture contributed equally to the total effect, it was now possible for a composition to consist of only two lines, melody and bass, the filling-in of the harmonies being left entirely to the *continuo* performer. With the increasing importance of the vocal and instrumental soloist, there appeared a new freedom of melodic invention and elaboration which had not previously been possible and which is directly attributable to the use of the *basso continuo* system.

The genius primarily responsible for transplanting this new style into Germany was Heinrich Schütz (1585-1672), who studied in Venice with Giovanni Gabrieli and later with Monteverdi, thus fully absorbing the Italian techniques. As early as 1623 Schütz composed one of the first German Oratorios, the *History of the Resurrection of Jesus Christ*, which was based on an earlier work by Antonio Scandello, and in 1627 the first German Opera, *Dafne*, the music of which is unfortunately lost. The *Resurrection History* reveals its modernity mainly in the use of an instrumental *continuo* accompaniment and in the boldness of its harmonic progressions. The narration of the Evangelist is in the old plainsong style and is in fact borrowed largely from the earlier work by Scandello; the words of Jesus are set for alto and tenor voices with *continuo* accompaniment, an impersonal method of representation which recalls the St John Passion (*c*. 1560) by Scandello, mentioned above. (See p. 25). In later life, Schütz produced three simple liturgical settings of the Passion story which are unequalled in dramatic expression by any save those of Bach.

From the seventeenth century onwards, Passion music became the peculiar concern of the Lutheran composers of north Germany. Gradually the novel features of the Italian Oratorio were adopted by these composers and wonderfully assimilated into an indigenous style. The plainsong narration of the ancient Dramatic Passion was replaced by the new recitative style, instrumental accompaniments were added, and lyrical movements in the form of arias, chorales, and orchestral symphonias were introduced to provide meditative commentary at significant points in the unfolding of the story. From this point in its history Passion composition started on the path of development which was to lead ultimately to the masterpieces of Bach.

In the succeeding chapters, the various works which illustrate this process of development will be examined in their appropriate contexts. As a basis for reference, however, it will be useful here to append a list of these Passion settings with their dates of composition and other relevant details:

1613	Melchior Vulpius	St Matthew Passion
1631	Christoph Demantius	St John Passion
1637	Thomas Mancinus	St Matthew Passion
1640	Thomas Selle	St John Passion (first setting for solo voices à 6, and choir à 5, without *Intermedia*)
1642	Thomas Selle	St Matthew Passion ('Passio in Dialogo secundum Matthaeum . . . im 10 Stimme')
1643	Thomas Selle	St John Passion (second setting for 6 vocal and 6 instrumental parts together with one vocal group à 5—'pro choro remoto'—and a chorus à 4)
1645	Heinrich Schütz	*The Seven Last Words from the Cross*
1653	Christoph Schultze	St Matthew Passion (music lost)
1664	Thomas Strutius	St Matthew Passion (music lost)
1664	Heinrich Schütz	St Luke Passion
1665	Heinrich Schütz	St John Passion
1666	Heinrich Schütz	St Matthew Passion
1667	Christian Flor	St Matthew Passion
?	Friedrich Funcke (attrib.)	St Matthew Passion (probably composed between 1667 and 1683)
1670	Augustin Pfleger	*The Seven Last Words from the Cross*
1672	Johann Sebastiani	St Matthew Passion

1673	Johann Theile	St Matthew Passion
c. 1683	Friedrich Funcke	St Luke Passion (music lost)
c. 1700	Johann Meder	St Matthew Passion
1700	Johann Kühnhausen	St Matthew Passion
1704	Reinhard Keiser	*Der blutige und sterbende Jesus* (The bleeding and dying Jesus). Passion libretto by Hunold-Menantes
1704	G. F. Handel	St John Passion. Libretto by Postel
1711	G. Böhm	St Luke Passion (music lost)
1711	Reinhard Keiser	*Tränen unter dem Kreuze Jesu* (Weeping under the Cross of Jesus). Passion libretto by König
1712	Reinhard Keiser	*Der für die Sünden der Welt gemarterte und sterbende Jesus* (Jesus martyred and dying for the sins of the world). Passion libretto by Brockes
1715	Reinhard Keiser	*Der zum Tode verurtheilte und gekreuzigte Jesus* (Jesus condemned to death and crucified). Passion libretto by König
1716	G. F. Handel	*Der für die Sünden der Welt gemarterte und sterbende Jesus* (Jesus, martyred and dying for the sins of the world). Passion libretto by Brockes.
1721	Johann Kuhnau	St Mark Passion
1722	G. P. Telemann	St Matthew Passion (the first in a series of 46 annual Passion settings written for Hamburg)

III

THE DRAMA

B Y far the majority of surviving Passions are settings of either St Matthew or St John. Even if we allow for the fact that in the course of time many early Passion compositions must have disappeared, there is still strong evidence of the favoured position held by these two Gospels. During the sixteenth century church composers doubtless gave preference to these particular accounts because of their traditional association with Palm Sunday and Good Friday which, as the principal days in Holy Week, naturally merited special musical celebrations. But such considerations will not suffice to explain the almost invariable choice of St Matthew's version by the Lutheran Oratorio Passion composers of the second half of the seventeenth century. At this period it was customary for elaborate musical settings of the Passion to be performed on Good Friday and composers were not normally restricted in their choice of the Gospel text to be set. It seems likely therefore that this striking preference for St Matthew's Gospel was to some extent prompted by purely artistic considerations arising from the differences in dramatic structure of the various accounts. As the new Oratorio type of Passion demanded a highly emotional and dramatic style of musical treatment, these composers turned naturally to the Gospel account which afforded the richest variety of incident. This, as we shall see, also helps to explain the significant neglect of St John's account by Passion composers at this time.

In its dramatic structure and its broad presentation of the various events in the story St Matthew's account in fact differs little from those in the other two synoptic Gospels (St Mark's and St Luke's), though in some respects it displays a greater richness of pictorial detail. It is for example the only Gospel to include the accounts of Judas's remorse and death, of the dream about Jesus which troubled Pilate's wife and of the governor's symbolical washing of his hands. St John's version, on the other hand, is strikingly different in construction as the continuous narrative of the Passion story begins in chapter eighteen with the arrest of Jesus at Gethsemane, and thus entirely omits the important preliminary scenes of the Last Supper and the Agony in the Garden. The account of the Last Supper does in fact appear in outline (without details of the Institution of the Holy Communion) in the thirteenth chapter of the Gospel, but this section is separated from the main body of the story by four interpolated chapters in which Jesus reveals to His disciples the coming redemption of the world by His death, and promises them the comfort of the Holy Spirit; in every case these earlier scenes were omitted entirely in musical settings of St John's account. Thus we can see that, of the two Gospel accounts favoured by ancient church tradition, St Matthew's displays a far richer and more balanced scheme of dramatic construction. This becomes immediately apparent if we make a direct comparison of the order of presentation of the main scenes in the two accounts:

St Matthew (ch. 26. 27)	*St John (ch. 18. 19)*
1. The chief priests seek to destroy Jesus	
2. Jesus is anointed with precious ointment	
3. Judas plans the betrayal	
4. The disciples prepare the Passover	
5. The Last Supper	
6. The Agony in the Garden	
7. The arrest of Jesus	1. The arrest of Jesus
8. The hearing before Caiaphas	2. Jesus is led before Annas
	3. Peter's denial (i)
9. Peter's denial and remorse	4. The hearing before Caiaphas
10. Judas's repentance and death	5. Peter's denial (ii)
11. The trial before Pilate	6. The trial before Pilate (i)
12. The soldiers, in mockery, crown Jesus with thorns	7. The soldiers mock Jesus
	8. The trial before Pilate (ii)
13. The Crucifixion. The death of Jesus and the earthquake	9. The Crucifixion. The death of Jesus

| 14. The descent from the Cross and the burial | 10. The descent from the Cross and the burial. |
| 15. The chief priests demand the sealing of the tomb | |

The truncation of the earlier scenes in St John's narrative is however offset by a considerable expansion of the scene of the trial before Pilate. In this account the Roman governor is represented as a tenacious character who is not unsympathetic to the cause of Jesus and not easily swayed by the importunity of the Jewish mob; as a result of this the people are more pressing in their demands and the scene contains nine vivid crowd utterances as compared with only four in St Matthew's version. As we shall see later when we come to consider Bach's setting of St John, this expansion of the trial scene, with its vivid depiction of the bitter enmity of Christ's accusers, affords outstanding opportunities to a composer for realistic and dramatic musical expression. Whereas in St Matthew's account there is a delicate balance between the devotional and dramatic elements, in St John's there is a sharp delineation of the more starkly tragic features of the story.

Nevertheless in spite of, or rather because of its vividly dramatic style, St John's account was not favoured by the seventeenth-century composers as it afforded relatively little scope for the use of one of the most characteristic features of the new Oratorio Passion form—the interpolation of meditative arias, *symphonias* and chorales. In construction the Oratorio Passion, like its ancient prototype the Dramatic Passion, consisted of a series of separate scenes (similar to the tableaux of a Mystery play) which were linked together by the impersonal 'past tense' narration of the Evangelist to form a logical sequence of events. In the Dramatic Passion the presentation of the story normally occurred without interruption, though the sectional nature of the composition provided opportunities for breaks between the scenes which could be used for prayer, meditation or a sermon.[1] Later in the development of the form such intervals were probably filled by

[1] One example is the interpolation of the Lord's Prayer after the scene of the death of Jesus in Johann Walter's St Matthew Passion (c. 1550) which was mentioned above. (See p. 25.)

musical meditations in the form of congregational chorales or instrumental music which would give the worshippers an opportunity to reflect actively or passively on the significance of the scenes which were being enacted before them. With the evolution of the Oratorio style these interpolations became increasingly important, were specially composed and printed in the score, and to a large extent determined the character of the work as a whole. There can be little doubt that the frequent choice of St Matthew's account by Oratorio Passion composers was prompted very largely by the excellent opportunities for such meditative commentary which occurred during the lengthy devotional scenes of the Last Supper and the Agony in the Garden.

Most of the German Oratorio Passions of the seventeenth century were divided (in imitation of the early Italian Oratorios) into two nearly equal parts, and in liturgical performance the interval between the two halves was occupied by a sermon on the subject of the Passion. The division in St Matthew's account was usually made after the scene of Peter's denial of Christ, a natural place for the break as it marks the end of the twenty-sixth chapter. The equivalent break in St John's version (at the end of the eighteenth chapter) occurs during the trial scene before Pilate after the crowd's cry 'Not this man, but Barabbas'. From the foregoing analysis of the structure of the Gospel stories, it will be obvious that St Matthew's account lends itself far more satisfactorily than St John's to such a bipartite arrangement. The two great scenes of the Last Supper and the Agony in the Garden form a complete section of a largely devotional nature which balances and contrasts well with the more urgently dramatic scenes of the Trial and the Crucifixion. St John's version, lacking this earlier section, will not readily divide into two halves of equal interest and importance; the choice here lies between a division which produces a short and uneventful first half and one which splits and weakens the highly dramatic trial scene. The difficulty of this problem is certainly another cogent reason for the neglect of St John's account. One of the few examples from this period, the second St John Passion (1643) by Thomas Selle, uses a much shortened version of the text and divides it into three sections, representing successively (i) the arrest of Jesus and the hearing before Caiaphas, (ii) the trial before Pilate, and (iii) the Crucifixion, which are separated by large-scale choral and orchestral movements (*Intermedia*), based on passages taken from the Old Testament. The abbreviation of the text and the tripartite construction suggest that Selle's model was the ancient Motet Passion rather than the contemporary Oratorio. As in the text of the Longaval Passion, the story is presented in three static word-pictures which are abstractions rather than flesh and blood representations, the vivid language of the Gospel being skilfully compressed into colourless and impersonal formulas.

The transitional stage between the Dramatic and the Oratorio types of Passion can be seen most clearly in the St Matthew Passion (1667) by Christian Flor, who was organist at the church of St Lambert and St John in Lüneburg. In its basic structure this setting is identical with the traditional Dramatic Passion. The Evangelist's narration and the sayings of the individual characters are set to a form of unaccompanied plainsong which was in fact borrowed entirely from an earlier Dramatic Passion by Melchior Vulpius, dating from 1613. The novelty of Flor's work lies in the use of an orchestra of flutes, viols and *continuo* to accompany the crowd choruses, and in the interpolation of numerous instrumental *symphonias* and vocal arias at focal points in the text. The Passion is divided into two parts, the first of which ends with the words of condemnation 'He is guilty of death' during the scene of the hearing before Caiaphas, followed by an alto aria based on the chorale *O Lamm Gottes unschuldig* (O guiltless Lamb of God). The great majority of Flor's meditative interpolations occur during the first half of the Passion; the scene of the Last Supper, for example, is broken by two arias and a *symphonia*, while the scene at Gethsemane (including the betrayal) is interrupted no less than seven times by *symphonias* and once by an aria. The numerous *symphonias* and solo arias in the first part of the work were doubtless intended to provide a musical balance for the many crowd choruses in the second half, though in the process of continual interruption the borrowed plainsong narration is disintegrated and tends to lose much of its artistic value. In later Oratorio Passions plainsong is replaced by recitative for the narration and purely instrumental movements tend to disappear; the meditative element is then supplied entirely by vocal arias, duets, and choruses, and by congregational chorales. But nevertheless, in Flor's setting we can see in embryo many of

37

the main structural features which are found in the Bach Passions.

When we turn to examine in more detail the two great Bach Passions, the importance of the differences in construction between St John's and St Matthew's accounts becomes even more obvious. The marked contrast which exists between the works is indeed largely attributable to the basic structural differences between these two Gospel versions. Each of the Passions is divided, in the accepted Oratorio tradition, into two parts; the break occurs in the St John Passion after the scene of Peter's denial and in the St Matthew Passion (departing from the usual custom) after the arrest of Jesus at Gethsemane. As a result of this division, the St John Passion has a very short first part, which is decidedly weak in dramatic incident and offers little scope to the composer for the introduction of lyrical meditative movements; thus the first half contains only three solo arias and four congregational chorales. Furthermore, the lack of crowd utterances in this part of the story is an additional hindrance to the composer in gaining a balanced musical scheme.

The first solo aria, 'Chains of bondage that I wrought me', sung by an alto, follows aptly enough upon the scene of the arrest of Jesus; but a weakness in the construction of the text is immediately apparent in the placing of the next aria, 'I follow in gladness to meet Thee', which is separated from the previous aria by only three bars of narration, '. . . and Simon Peter followed Jesus, and so did another disciple.' Apart from the excessive crowding of the lyrical element at this point, the joyous character of this second aria is singularly inappropriate as a commentary upon the approaching faithlessness of Peter.

In the scene of Peter's interrogation by the onlookers in the courtyard there is further evidence of the difficulty which Bach experienced in maintaining a formal balance in this Passion. In an attempt to compensate for the lack of crowd utterances in this part of the work, the composer expands the chorus 'Art thou not one of his disciples?' into a movement of seventeen bars, with forty-six repetitions of the words 'Art thou not'. The effect is forced and artificial; how simple and yet how brilliantly effective is the setting of the same section in the St Matthew Passion ('Surely, thou also art one of them for thy speech bewrayeth thee'), in which four bars of music with practically no word-repetition suffice to paint the scene in the most vivid terms.

St John's version of the scene of Peter's denial differs from St Matthew's by its omission of the deeply affecting words of remorse '. . . and he went out and wept bitterly.' Similarly at the end of his account of the Passion, in the scene of the death of Christ, there is no mention of the earthquake and the opening of the graves. Such pictorial touches, though of little intrinsic importance, do afford considerable opportunities to a dramatic composer for expressive musical treatment and the lack of these imaginative details may in fact provide a further reason for the neglect of St John's account by the majority of Oratorio Passion composers. Indeed it is difficult to account for Bach's choice of this text for his first great Passion composition, unless, as has been suggested,[1] he was specifically directed by the church authorities at Leipzig to produce a setting of this particular Gospel. Bach, however, does not hesitate to compensate for the lack of dramatic climaxes by boldly importing both the incidents mentioned above into the text of his St John Passion. In his anxiety to make dramatic capital out of the episode of Peter's remorse, the composer in fact tends to overreach himself and, with a long and exaggerated *melisma* on the word 'wept', produces a highly artificial effect, which contrasts poorly with the much simpler but more heart-searchingly expressive setting in the St Matthew Passion.

The weaknesses of construction in the first part of the St John Passion are due partly to the basic structure of the Gospel account and partly to the composer's lack, at the time of composition, of a skilled literary collaborator. As we have seen in the first chapter, the composition of this Passion occupied Bach during the winter months immediately preceding his appointment, in the spring of 1723, as Cantor at St Thomas's; at this time he had yet to establish contact with Picander, his principal librettist. Bach was thus forced to borrow his lyrical material piecemeal from several sources, the chief of which was the popular Passion libretto *Der für die Sünden der Welt gemarterte und sterbende Jesus* (Jesus, martyred and dying for the sins of the world), by Heinrich Brockes, a text which had previously been set by many of the Hamburg Opera composers, notably Keiser and Handel. The actual adaptation of this borrowed material and the construc-

[1] C. S. Terry, *The St John Passion*, O.U.P., 1928, p. 12.

tion of the libretto was very probably the work of Bach himself.

The scene of the trial before Pilate, which begins the second part of the work, is wonderfully effective. Here Bach's problems of construction are solved by the Gospel narrative itself and the nine crowd choruses, set with splendid vividness and imagination, follow each other in practically unbroken succession. Each chorus is a fairly lengthy and elaborate musical composition and, linked together by the terse narrative of the Evangelist, they form a dramatic scene of great power and vitality; the comparative absence of lyrical commentary can here be regarded as a positive asset. The most substantial point of meditative repose in this scene occurs after the scourging of Jesus, an obvious dramatic climax, where the bass arioso 'Come, ponder, O my soul' and the tenor aria 'Behold Him: see, His back all torn and bleeding' provide an effective relaxation of tension which helps to throw the continuation of the dramatic scene into sharp relief.

A curious feature of the trial scene in the St John Passion lies in the occasional use of the same music for two different choruses. The music of 'We have a law', for example, reappears (a semitone lower) in the succeeding chorus 'If thou let this man go, thou art not Caesar's friend.' It is possible that Bach intended this device of repetition to impart unity to his musical scheme, though the use of the same music for the two choruses 'Hail, thou King of the Jews'—an expression of mockery, and 'Write not thou, the King of the Jews'—an expression of outraged protest, seems to be an error of judgment. Terry[1] ingeniously explains this as a subtlety on the part of Bach; the Jews who were willing enough to hail Jesus as their king in mockery are less prepared to accept the title, 'King of the Jews', as a superscription over the Cross; by means of the musical repetition, the composer draws attention to their inconsistency. The most probable explanation is however simple and practical; there were many occasions in Bach's life when the pressure on his time overtaxed even his extraordinary capacity for original work, and at such times, the music for a new work would be borrowed and adapted from some earlier composition.[2] As we have seen

[1] C. S. Terry, op. cit., pp. 43-44.
[2] See p. 14.

earlier, it was under such pressure that the St John Passion was produced, as Bach wished to have the work ready for performance at the beginning of his tenure of office at Leipzig. The 'borrowings' in the Passion are from within the work itself and are by no means ineffective.[1]

In the final Crucifixion scene, Bach was again faced with a difficult problem of construction, as St John's narrative contains only one crowd utterance at the foot of the Cross. In order to preserve the balance of his musical structure, the composer is forced to make a disproportionately long and elaborate movement out of the trivial words of the soldiers, squabbling over the division of Christ's garments, 'Let us not divide it but cast lots for it'. The solemn character of this final scene is marked by a generous provision of lyrical movements, three congregational chorales and four solo arias. In the tenor arioso 'My heart, behold the world intent a share in Jesu's pain to borrow', which follows the earthquake scene interpolated from St Matthew's Gospel, there is a slight textual inconsistency which again reveals Bach's difficulty with his lyrical material. The stanza, which is adapted from Brockes's Passion text, tells how the natural world is also affected by the sorrowful events, and refers in particular to the shrouding of the sun's beams (*Die Sonne sich in Trauer kleidet*). But the composer appears to have overlooked the fact that there is no mention in St John's account (nor in the account of the earthquake inserted here from St Matthew's Gospel) of the 'darkness over the whole land'.[2]

The greatness of the St John Passion lies in the vivid, visual realism of its dramatic presentation of the story. By means of the sharply drawn contrast between the fanatical fury of the crowd and the spiritual calm and detachment of Christ, Bach achieves a powerful and imaginative interpretation of the Gospel tragedy in which a strong link is retained with the religious dramas of medieval times. Disunity in the musical structure arises, as we have seen, mainly from the composer's attempt to make an unsuitable text conform entirely to the conventions of the contemporary Oratorio style with its

[1] An interesting parallel case occurs in the B minor Mass, where the music of the *Gratias Agimus* is repeated exactly in *Dona nobis pacem*; in this case, however, Bach is clearly concerned with preserving the unity of his structure.

[2] See Matt. 27.45, Mark 15.33, Luke 23.45, the last of which specifically refers to the darkening of the sun.

bipartite construction and its liberal use of meditative commentary. It is particularly in the uneasy fusion of religious contemplation with vivid liturgical drama that we find elements which are disruptive of Bach's artistic scheme. The strength of the St Matthew Passion, on the other hand, lies more in its epic devotional qualities than in its dramatic realism. Aided by the rich variety of incident in St Matthew's account, and by the skilled collaboration of the versatile Picander, Bach was able to produce a work of beautifully balanced proportions, in which the lyrical interpolations are blended with the Gospel drama to achieve a perfect artistic unity. The method of construction, in which the ancient Dramatic Passion origins are easily traceable, is that of a series of short dramatic tableaux, interspersed at significant points with devotional meditations. In the majority of cases the reflective arias, unlike those in the St John Passion, are preceded by short arioso recitatives which comment directly upon the scene which has just been enacted and thus provide a link between the dramatic narrative and the purely lyrical aria; an interesting example of the way in which Bach could use a simple musical convention (the recitative and aria) for an important structural purpose. The placing of the chorales in relation to the text, probably the work of Bach himself, is, as we shall see later, particularly apt. The great Passion hymn O Haupt voll Blut und Wunden (O sacred Head), by Paul Gerhardt, appears five times at points of climax in the narrative—(i) after Christ's words 'I will smite the shepherd', foretelling His desertion by the disciples, (ii) after Peter's vow of fidelity, (iii) after the scene during the trial before Pilate, where Jesus is silent before His accusers, (iv) after the scene where Jesus is mocked by the soldiers and crowned with thorns, and (v) after the death of Jesus. The fivefold repetition of Hassler's famous melody, which is set to this hymn, imparts a considerable degree of musical unity to the work as a whole.

The two great scenes of the Last Supper and the Agony in the Garden, which form the substance of the first part of the work, both afford ample opportunity for devotional meditation; but, in contrast to the practice of the earlier seventeenth-century composers (such as Christian Flor), who break these scenes with numerous short interpolations, Bach restricts himself to a few long and highly-developed meditative movements.

Thus the scene of the Last Supper is interrupted only ...
by a chorale which follows the disciples' questioning chorus
'Lord, is it I?', and by a soprano recitative and aria which
follows the Institution of the Holy Communion. Similarly the
scene at Gethsemane is broken only three times by lyrical
interpolations, two lengthy recitatives and arias (one each for
the tenor and bass soloists) and a congregational chorale.

The crowd choruses in the second half of the work lack
the demoniacal intensity of those in the earlier Passion, and,
despite such brilliant dramatic strokes as the single simul-
taneous shout of 'Barabbas', the trial scene is painted in less
vividly realistic terms. Continually, reflective solos of ethereal
beauty are intermingled with the Gospel narrative, thereby
softening the impact of the tragedy and preserving the meditative, devotional character of the work as a whole. At one
point, where Pilate's question 'Why, what evil hath He done?'
is followed by a long recitative and aria 'To all men Jesus
good hath done', the dramatic continuity is all but lost;
doubtless Picander found the temptation to answer Pilate's
question directly with an account of Christ's good deeds hard
to resist.

St Matthew's account, unlike St John's, provides for five
crowd choruses at the foot of the Cross, and, in this series,
Bach shows consummate skill and psychological insight. The
first two choruses 'Thou that destroyest the Temple' and 'He
saved others, Himself He cannot save' are delivered by a
double chorus in quick succession and with a fanatical
vehemence reminiscent of the great St John choruses. The
next two choruses, 'He calleth for Elias' and 'Let be, let us
see whether Elias will come to save Him', which follow the
account of the 'darkness over all the land' and of Jesus's
despairing cry 'Eli, Eli, lama sabachthani', are for single choir
only; gone is the mood of mockery and ribaldry and, in its
place, there is one of awe and half-belief. Finally, after the
earthquake which follows the scene of the death of Christ,
this tendency towards belief is confirmed in the chorus 'Truly
this was the Son of God', one of the supreme moments in the
work. The performance of the Passion at Leipzig is known to
have taken place at a Vespers service which began in the early
afternoon of Good Friday and which must have lasted until
fairly late in the evening. The twilight and approaching darkness at the end of the performance were undoubtedly well

suited to Bach's expressive scheme in the St Matthew Passion, as is evident in the gradual darkening of the vocal and instrumental colouring in the final scenes. The sole interruption to this general plan lies in the violent chorus addressed by the chief priests and the Pharisees to Pilate, 'Sir, we remember that that deceiver said, while He was yet alive— after three days I will rise again'; this was possibly an unwelcome intrusion for the composer as a disrupting element which would not fit in with his overall conception. In an elaborately contrapuntal chorus, the priests argue themselves from the opening key of E flat major to a final cadence in D minor, a very unusual procedure for Bach.

This brief analysis of the two Bach Passions will suffice to show their marked differences in dramatic structure. Whereas the St John Passion represents an idealized form of the ancient liturgical Dramatic type of Passion, the St Matthew breaks new ground as a mystical musical meditation which is based on the Oratorio style but which is primarily non-dramatic in conception. The musical techniques employed in both the works are virtually identical; recitative for the Gospel narration; terse, dramatic choral writing for the crowd utterances; and chorales and richly accompanied arias, duets and choruses to supply the meditative element. In the succeeding chapters, we shall turn to examine these various techniques in more detail and to trace their gradual evolution from primitive origins.

IV

THE DRAMATIS PERSONAE

THE small group of Florentine musicians, poets and philosophers who, at the beginning of the seventeenth century, began to fashion a new theory of art, were, as we have seen earlier, inspired by what they mistakenly believed to have been the ideals of classical Greece. According to these supposed ideals, which were fully consistent with the humanistic spirit of the age, music was the complement of poetry, its servant and its choicest ornament; the natural and highest function of the art was to illuminate and heighten the emotional power of verse. In classical drama, so it was thought, pure vocal melody had been carefully fashioned to follow the rhythms and metres of the text, thereby achieving a harmonious union of poetry and music, a perfect balance of form and expression which had since been lost in the crudities and artificial complexities of choral polyphony. The most important outcome of these theories was the development of a new means of dramatic expression, the *stile rappresentativo* (the theatrical style), in which a solo voice with simple instrumental accompaniment attempted to reproduce melodically the accents and inflexions of rhetorical speech. The first essays in this new style, the monodies and short musical dramas of composers such as Peri and Caccini, were frequently formless, rhapsodical and, by modern standards, exceedingly tedious; but from these primitive beginnings there sprang a whole new conception of the relationship of music to drama. The *stile rappresentativo*, in a more highly organized form, had two important offshoots, the recitative and the aria, both of which were destined to play a leading rôle in the development of the new Opera and Oratorio forms.

The growth of this new theatrical technique had an obvious importance in the development of Passion composition; now, for the first time, it became possible for the narrative and descriptive words of the Evangelist and the dramatic utterances of the individual characters to be set to music in a realistic manner in which the accents and rhythms of human speech could be not only reproduced but also enhanced by the contour of the vocal line. This new style was to replace the centuries-old tradition whereby plainchant was always used for the sayings of the various characters in the drama. The traditional plainsong used for the Passion is of great antiquity and consequently very simple in style; usually the greater part of a sentence is set to a single reciting-note which is preceded by a short rising phrase of intonation and followed by a falling cadence formula. It would however be a mistake to confuse artistic values with complexity of method. Plainsong reached perfection as a mature and finished art over a thousand years ago and is unsurpassed as the fulfilment of a liturgical ideal. In Passion composition, the substitution of recitative for plainsong should not be regarded as an artistic improvement but rather as a new orientation of the means of dramatic expression.

A comparison of the principal features of plainsong and recitative, particularly in their relation to Passion music, will reveal the extent of the dramatic capabilities inherent in the latter technique. In the first place, plainsong was designed solely for liturgical purposes and was thus necessarily impersonal and ritualistic in style; recitative on the other hand grew from secular, theatrical origins and was intended as a vehicle for strong personal emotion and vivid naturalism. In plainsong, phrases and sentences were set to rigidly constructed musical formulas which, though of considerable intrinsic beauty, paid little direct heed to the ideas and emotions expressed by the words;[1] but in recitative, the music would attempt to stress symbolically the emotional colouring of complete sentences and to 'paint' by means of melodic and harmonic equivalents the pictorial images suggested by individual words. The attainment of such dramatic and expressive ends in recitative was assisted by the use of a wide and flexible vocal range as opposed to the narrow compass of plainsong; and by the use of rests, rhetorical pauses, and vivid

---

[1] A single exception to this can be found in the plainsong setting of Christ's words '*Eli, Eli, lama sabachthani*' where the voice-part achieves expressive realism by rising above its normal pitch to an unnaturally shrill tone.

rhythmic contrasts as compared with the smooth continuous flow of the earlier technique. In plainsong again, the reciting-note method of declamation contained no precise indications of rhythm and the singer was consequently free to reproduce in a formal manner the accents of natural speech; in recitative, on the other hand, an attempt was made to imitate the pitch inflexions of the speaking voice and this of course necessitated a much more precise musical notation of the rhythm. In this connection it is important to remember that, while plainsong was designed for the musical presentation of a ritual language,[1] recitative was fashioned for the infinitely more difficult task of presenting the inflexions of a living tongue. Finally, while plainsong was essentially unaccompanied melody, recitative was incomplete without the harmonic support of the *continuo*, and in consequence recitative, unlike plainsong, was subject to definite harmonic laws and thus capable of such expressive and structural devices as modulation from one key to another.

The stereotyped nature of the plainsong in the ancient Passions may be judged from the fact that fixed formulas were used for the beginnings and endings of phrases in the various voice-parts. The different phrase-endings were in fact designed to indicate which of the characters was next in turn to speak; thus, for example, the cadence formula in the Evangelist's part which was used to introduce the words of Christ differed from the one which preceded the utterances of the crowd. Similarly, a simple cadence ending, consisting of four notes ascending step-wise to the final, was used very frequently to signify the presence of a question-mark.[2] It is interesting to compare this abstract representation of the verbal question in plainsong with the normal recitative treatment in which the actual upward leap of the questioning voice is reproduced melodically in the voice-part with a resulting vividness of effect. In the following example, two settings of the same passage from St Matthew's Gospel, one in plainsong (Melchior Vulpius— 1613) and the other in recitative (J. S. Bach—1729) are set side by side for comparison; this shows clearly the graphic nature of the new style.

---

[1] After the Reformation, plainsong was adapted for use with the vernacular, notably in the German settings of the Passion; but this in no way affects its basic function.

[2] See O. Kade, *Die ältere Passionskomposition bis zum Jahre 1631*, Gütersloh, 1893, pp. 2-4.

Example 1   (a) *St Matthew Passion* (1613)   M. Vulpius
             (b) *St Matthew Passion* (1729)   J. S. Bach

(Trans: Could ye not watch with Me one hour? Watch and
pray that ye enter not into temptation.)

We can see here many of the essential features in which
recitative differs from plainsong; emotional colouring, wide
melodic range, realistic representation of the question, rhetorical pauses, and a melodic line which attempts to follow the
natural inflexions of the speaking voice. This extract from
Bach shows of course a fully mature type of recitative which
differs considerably from the primitive declamation of the
early monodic composers; but nevertheless it follows all the
basic principles of the early theorists.

The use of cadence formulas in plainsong, mentioned above,
was later paralleled in recitative by a similar device which
sprang from a natural desire to impose some degree of formal
organization on to the rhapsodical declamation of the *stile
rappresentativo*. In this formula, which came to be regarded

48

as an elaborate type of musical punctuation, the end of a sentence was usually marked by a fall of a fourth (from tonic to dominant) in the voice-part, which was immediately answered by a perfect cadence (dominant to tonic) played on the accompanying instrument. At one place in the St John Passion, Bach is betrayed by the use of this formula into a somewhat perfunctory setting of part of one of the Seven Last Words from the Cross—'Behold, thy mother'. Intrinsically the phrase is shapely and beautiful; the perfunctoriness results of course from the unhappy marriage of highly significant words to a musical cliché.

In addition to its simple function as a realistic method of reproducing speech, recitative was capable of a wide range of expressive effects in which the emotional colouring of particular words would be underlined by symbolical means. This type of 'word-painting' is an important feature of Bach's recitative style; there are for instance several places in the Passions where the Evangelist abandons his normal rôle as a detached story-teller and gives expression to his personal feelings about the events which he is describing. This subjective style of narration is usually achieved by means of a vocal *melisma* which 'paints' expressively and symbolically the significant word in the passage. In the following example, the tortured contours of the vocal *melisma* set to the word 'crucified' graphically illustrate the narrator's feelings about the agonies of crucifixion.

Example 2   *St John Passion* (1723)   J. S. Bach

A further, more subtle method of underlining the emotional impact of particular words was by the use of discords or chromatic harmonies played on the accompanying *continuo* instrument. Frequently a word such as 'betrayed' would appear in the voice-part without any special expressive treatment; but the narrator's feeling of shame and horror would be subtly portrayed by the dark colouring of a discord, such as the diminished seventh, in the accompaniment. As we shall see later when we come to examine Bach's expressive harmonization of chorale melodies, the diminished seventh was Bach's favourite chord for underlining the meaning of such words as 'pain', 'fear', 'sorrow', and 'death'; in the example from the St John Passion given above, the first four notes of the *melisma* on 'crucified' form the arpeggio of a diminished seventh chord which is actually played at the same time in the accompaniment.

In some cases, particularly in the St John Passion, Bach's search for an expressive, pictorial vocal line resulted in effects which are artificial and exaggerated. A typical example is the setting of the word 'wept' in the scene of Peter's denial, which was mentioned in the last chapter (see p. 39). There are even occasions when the composer transfers features of the keyboard style of the period to the solo vocal part in an attempt to colour the meaning of particular words. In the next example, we can see, in the setting of the word 'scourged', the typical figuration of a harpsichord fantasia and, in the setting of the word 'fight', the characteristic rhetorical gesture of the organ pedals in some great prelude, fantasia, or toccata.

Example 3   *St John Passion* (1723)   J. S. Bach

In the St Matthew Passion, vocal *melisma* is used in a much more restrained manner and its effect is consequently more deeply moving and expressive.

An interesting transitional stage between plainsong and recitative can be seen in the St John Passion (1643) by the

Hamburg Cantor Thomas Selle (1599-1663). In this work, the words of the Evangelist, Jesus and the minor characters are elaborately accompanied by various combinations of instruments in an attempt at musical characterization. Some apt effects are achieved; in the accompaniment to the words of Pilate, for instance, cornetti and trombones are used to emphasize the pomp and circumstance which surround the Roman governor. The vocal line of the recitative is similar in style to plainsong with its use of long reciting-notes and formal cadences; but owing to the presence of complicated rhythms in the instrumental accompaniment, the characteristic flexibility of plainsong declamation is inevitably lacking and the effect is cramped and inexpressive. This is particularly noticeable in the lengthy narrative sections where the voice of the Evangelist is accompanied by a strange instrumental combination consisting of two bassoons with harpsichord and 'cello *continuo*. This tendency to restrict the freedom of the vocal declamation by the use of overloaded accompaniments can be seen in many of the later seventeenth-century Passions. A good instance is the setting of St Matthew's account (1673) by Johann Theile of Lübeck, where the viols which are consistently used to accompany the words of the Evangelist decorate the harmonic background to the recitative with intricate arpeggio figures. True freedom in vocal declamation is only possible against the very simplest chordal accompaniment on the *continuo*. This can be seen in the St Matthew Passion (*c*. 1700) by Johann Meder, where a very sensitively constructed type of recitative flows easily and naturally against the long sustained chords of the organ *continuo*.

Thomas Selle's elaborate system of characterization by instrumental accompaniment is not met with in any other early Passion composition; there is in fact no other work of this period which uses such lavish orchestral resources.[1] It was, however, the normal practice to underline the sombre sweetness of Jesus's words by the addition of an accompaniment for violins; a sublime survival of this custom is to be found in Bach's St Matthew Passion. In Sebastiani's setting of St Matthew (1672), there is an interesting anticipation of one of Bach's most imaginative touches; in the setting of the words ' *Eli, Eli, lama sabachthani* ', the violins, which are normally used to accompany the words of Jesus, are temporarily silent

[1] See p. 104.

and the *continuo* alone supplies the harmonic background. This temporary silencing of the string tone symbolizes in a wonderful manner the despair and humiliation of the Saviour at this moment of greatest trial.

Apart from such instrumental delineation, the usual means of characterization in Passion music was by the use of voices of contrasting pitch and colouring. As we have seen earlier, the traditional voices used in the Plainsong Passion were a bass for the part of Jesus, a tenor for the Evangelist, and an alto for all the other characters, including the crowd. Throughout the long history of the development of the form, every Passion composer (including Bach) was content to leave the Evangelist as a tenor[1] and, with one important exception which will be discussed later, Jesus as a bass; but the continual search for greater realism brought about many changes in the voice-characterization of the minor rôles. The gradual tendency of composers during the century before Bach was to raise the voice-pitch of the female characters and lower that of the male characters, thus producing a sharper distinction between the sexes and also a voice-colouring which was more nearly in conformity with the popular conception of the various persons in the drama.[2] Thus we find, in Bach's St Matthew Passion, that only two very subsidiary characters, the first false witness and the second maid, are represented by the traditional alto voice; the four important male characters —Judas, Peter, Caiaphas and Pilate—are all set as basses, while the principal female characters, Pilate's wife and the first maid, are sopranos whose short passages of recitative are pitched fairly high. An intermediate stage in this development can be seen in the St Matthew Passion (1666) by Schütz, where Judas and Pilate's wife are represented by an alto, Peter and Pilate by a tenor, and Caiaphas by a bass. Occasionally, even as late as the early eighteenth century, we come across curious reminders of the ancient *synagoga* tradition, such as the representation of Pilate by an alto voice in Handel's St John Passion of 1704.

Except for this general distinction between the various

[1] A single exception to this is found in the St John Passion by Alessandro Scarlatti (1660-1725) in which the part of the *Testo* (Narrator) is written for a counter-tenor.

[2] A notable curiosity, which occurs in a sixteenth-century setting (the St Matthew Passion, 1534, by Claudin de Sermisy), is the representation of Pilate's wife by four *male* voices!

characters which is created by differences of vocal pitch, little attempt is normally made in Passion music at detailed musical characterization. Only the part of Christ stands out by virtue of its gravity and gentleness. Doubtless, even in the most advanced operatic types of Passion composition, a really theatrical degree of musical characterization was considered unsuitable and irreverent. Nevertheless, subtle touches abound; typical is the presentation of the testimony of the false witnesses in canonic imitation. Considerable variety is shown in the choice of the interval which separates the canonic parts, the fourth and the fifth being the most commonly used; but the most realistic version is undoubtedly the one in Schütz's St Matthew Passion where the conflict in the testimony of the witnesses is amusingly parodied by the use of canon at the second.

Example 4   *St Matthew Passion* (1666)   H. Schütz

(Trans.: He has said, I can destroy the Temple of God)

Mention was made above of a single exception to the traditional use of the bass voice for the representation of Christ. This occurs in a composition by Schütz entitled *The Seven Last Words from the Cross* in which the utterances of Christ are allotted to a tenor voice. It is not easy to discover

Schütz's motives for making this change from the accepted tradition, though it seems possible that, as this work was designed as an essay in the new emotional Italian style, exploiting the expressive possibilities of the solo vocal recitative with instrumental accompaniment, the composer chose the tenor voice because of its outstandingly rich and expressive timbre. The *Seven Last Words*, which was composed in 1645, is not a strict liturgical Passion but rather a short type of Oratorio based on a compilation in German from all four Gospels which presents the 'Seven Words' in a logical sequence. The libretto is thus clearly modelled on the Latin Motet Passion texts of the Renaissance period, which, it will be remembered, similarly presented the seven last utterances of Christ in their final sections. The provenance of the 'Seven Last Words' and their order of appearance in the work is as follows:

    (i) From St Luke: 'Father, forgive them; for they know not what they do'.
    (ii) From St John: 'Woman, behold thy son! . . . Behold, thy Mother!'
    (iii) From St Luke: 'Verily, I say unto thee, to-day thou shalt be with Me in Paradise'.
    (iv) From St Matthew and St Mark: 'Eli, Eli, lama sabachthani'.
    (v) From St John: 'I thirst'.
    (vi) From St John: 'It is finished'.
    (vii) From St Luke: 'Father, into Thy hands I commend My Spirit'.

In Schütz's setting, the actual Gospel narrative is framed in two five-part choruses (Introitus and Conclusio) which are accompanied by the *continuo*; the text for both these choruses is taken from the Passion hymn *Da Jesus an dem Kreuze stund* by Johann Böschenstein, but no use is made of the traditional music of the chorale. Within this vocal framework there is a further one for an orchestra of unspecified instruments, which performs a solemn *symphonia*, once after the opening chorus and again, repeated exactly, before the final chorus. The seven utterances from the Cross are linked together by short sections of narrative which are freely adapted from all four Gospels. These narrative passages are not entrusted to one

54

single voice throughout, but are variously presented by a tenor, a soprano, an alto and, on three occasions, by a complete four-part chorus, accompanied in each case by the *continuo* only. A highly expressive recitative style is used for the words of Jesus, with rhetorical word-repetitions and dramatic pauses which were doubtless intended to depict the agonized gasps of the dying Saviour. The emotional effect of this music, which is enhanced by the use of an ethereal accompaniment (probably for stringed instruments) and by simple but expressive harmonies, can be judged from the following short example:

Example 5   *The Seven Last Words* (1645)   H. Schütz

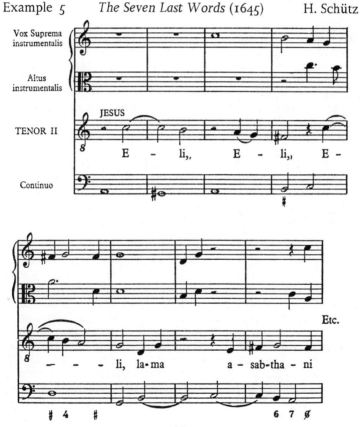

The *Seven Last Words* is a work of grave beauty which in numerous felicitous touches and, in particular, in the expressive flexibility of its vocal lines reveals the mastery of its author. One later imitation survives. This is a setting of a very similar text, dating from 1670, by Augustin Pfleger, then Capellmeister at Gottorf. Pfleger reverts to the normal use of the bass voice for the part of Christ. His text, a compilation from all four Gospels, is clearly modelled on Schütz's though it is shortened considerably by abbreviations and omissions; the first of the utterances from the Cross, for example, is given as ' *Vergib ihnen, denn sie wissen nicht, was sie tun* ' (Forgive them, for they know not what they do), thus omitting the important opening word 'Father'. But in conformity with the growing custom of the period Pfleger expands his work by the insertion of a number of lyrical verses, one appearing after each of the ' Seven Words'; these lyrical interpolations are set in a rather sentimental Italianate style for soprano and alto, singing mainly in parallel thirds. The text also includes, rather strangely, the account (from St John) of the writing of the superscription over the Cross and the crowd chorus which follows ' Write thou not, The King of the Jews'. At the beginning of the work there is a short orchestral *symphonia* for viols and *continuo* which is followed immediately by a lengthy dialogue for soprano and bass, a setting of words taken from the twenty-third chapter of St Luke : ' Daughters of Jerusalem, weep not for Me, but weep for yourselves and for your children.' And at the end of the work there is a *concertato* setting (a setting for combined voices and instruments) of the famous Passion chorale *O Lamm Gottes unschuldig* (O guiltless Lamb of God). But in spite of its elaborate construction Pfleger's work is on purely musical grounds much inferior to Schütz's; whereas the creative mind of Schütz was able to absorb the new Italian style and re-fashion it into a personal mode of expression, the lesser talent of Pfleger was capable only of producing a weak imitation of the Italian manner. In Pfleger's setting of the actual words of Christ we find a much less emotional style of recitative than in Schütz; there is, for instance, no sign of the emotive repetition of phrases and the expressive pauses which characterize the earlier work. Pfleger's recitative belongs to an intermediate period between the extravagant rhetorical manner of the earlier *stile rappresentativo*, which Schütz uses with restraint and great effectiveness, and the beautifully modelled 'natural speech' type of declamation which we find in the works of Keiser, Handel and Bach in the early eighteenth century. As in the works of Sebastiani and Theile, which also belong to this intermediate period, the recitative of Jesus, being for a bass voice, is closely linked to the bass of the *continuo* accompaniment and only occasionally rises above it. The difficult problem of achieving independence between the vocal line and the *continuo* arises most urgently in the case of bass recitative and this may well be one reason why the earlier Oratorio Passion composers avoid using the bass voice for the portrayal of the minor male characters.

In view of the extreme adventurousness of Schütz's setting of the *Seven Last Words*, it is surprising to find in his liturgical Passion music, which was composed twenty years later, an apparent reversion to an archaic style; in every outward respect, these three Passions, St Luke (1664), St John (1665), and St Matthew (1666), are Dramatic Passions of the traditional type: mock plainsong is used for the words of narration, accompanying instruments are dispensed with, and concerted vocal music is used only in the settings of the crowd utterances and in the opening and final choruses. The great German master who in his youth had so ardently championed the new Italian style of composition, now reverts, perhaps in disillusionment after the bitter experiences of the Thirty Years' War, to the simple traditional style of church composition. It is quite possible that the composer foresaw how great a menace to German art there lay in the facile attractions of the Italian Opera style; we find for example that in his old age he urged all young German musicians to lay the foundations of their work on the strong contrapuntal techniques of the past.

A closer examination of the recitative in the Schütz Passions reveals however that the composer has not merely imitated the old plainchant style of declamation, but has in fact invented an entirely new type of unaccompanied speech-song of a flexible and highly expressive character. The notation of this recitative gives no indication of rhythm except to show by means of a long note-value (a kind of musical semi-colon) the various points of repose in a phrase or sentence; consequently the singer is free, as in plainsong, to reproduce the natural rhythms of speech. But the skill of the composer is everywhere apparent in the delicately moulded fluctuations of pitch and in the short *melismas* which fit perfectly with the natural flow of the words and underline expressively or dramatically the meaning of the text. A notable example occurs in the St Matthew Passion where, in the setting of Judas's words '*Was wollt ihr mir geben? Ich will ihn euch verraten*' (What will ye give me, and I will deliver Him unto you?), we find one of the most brilliant pieces of musical characterization in any Passion before Bach. The words 'what will ye give me?' are sung twice to a short musical phrase which rises sequentially and are followed by an urgent repetition of the word 'I', thus giving a remarkably vivid impression of greed and covetousness; the whole passage is a masterly little character-sketch, achieved by the simplest of means.

A proper study of this style of recitative would involve a host of musical examples and an attention to detail which is beyond the scope of this short book. It must suffice here to draw attention to the most impressive feature of Schütz's style—the sureness of his technique. In these great Passion settings, the composer is working with the simplest of musical materials; and yet, despite the austerity of the medium, there is never the least indication of any restraint on his creative imagination and every detail of the musical conception is moulded with the greatest care to form perfectly shaped works of art. There is no better illustration of the fact, mentioned earlier in connection with plainsong, that artistic values are quite independent of complexity of technique.

The final stage in the development of recitative before Bach can be seen in the work of the great Hamburg Opera composer Reinhard Keiser (1674-1739). In addition to his numerous Operas, this extraordinarily gifted composer produced several settings of the poetic Passion librettos which were popular in Hamburg at the turn of the century. In their flawless declamation and rhythmic sensitivity, the recitatives of Keiser are closely allied to those of Bach and Handel. Particularly striking is his use of an *arioso* type of declamation in which the speech rhythms of pure recitative begin to flower into lyrical song. Many instances of the use of this *arioso* technique are to be found in the Bach Passions, particularly in the setting of the Institution of the Holy Communion from the St Matthew Passion where Christ's words are united with lyrical music of compelling sincerity and aptness.

Apart from the occasional exaggerated and artificial passages in the St John Passion noticed above, Bach's use of operatic recitative for the sayings of the various characters in the drama is normally marked by dignity and restraint; realism of expression is consistently achieved without any lowering of musical standards and without recourse to purely theatrical effects. It is interesting to notice that the recitative sections which are followed by lyrical movements invariably end with a formal perfect cadence, whereas those which lead directly into the dramatic crowd utterances avoid such finality and achieve greater vividness by musical continuity. The most striking example of this dramatic use of continuity occurs in the trial scene from the St Matthew Passion where the normal cadence formula on the *continuo* which follows the Evangelist's introductory words ' they said ' is brilliantly interrupted by the harsh, discordant shout of ' Barabbas ' from the crowd. The simple device of the interrupted cadence, a normal feature of harmonic technique from early times, is here used for a specifically dramatic purpose and creates with a single imaginative stroke a vivid and expressive musical picture.

V

THE CROWD

THE history of the development of Passion composition is of course closely allied to the history of the evolution of musical technique as a whole; as music gradually acquired new resources for dramatic and emotional expression there was naturally a parallel increase of dramatic realism in musical settings of the Passion story. But a further important influence on the growth of the Passion form is apparent in the constant interaction of sacred and secular elements, in the process of cross-fertilization which emphasizes in turn the theatrical realism required by popular taste and the ritual mysticism demanded by church tradition. Thus we find that, in the Middle Ages, the ritual chanting of the Passion story gave rise to secular Passion plays, in which the theatrical element was freely developed, and that these plays, in their turn, instituted changes in the liturgical office by encouraging more realistic methods of presentation.

Fundamentally, all church ritual springs from a natural dramatic instinct; but the expression of this instinct in the church liturgy is usually abstract and symbolical in character. In liturgical Passion music however the inherent drama is of a very different nature; the directness and vividness of style is in this case predetermined by the dramatic nature of the Gospel narratives. But nevertheless, even in the settings of the Passion, the natural conservatism of church ritual continually exercised a restraining influence on the growth of theatrical realism and ensured a degree of impersonal detachment in the presentation of the sacred drama.

The realistic dramatic elements in Bach's Passion music are drawn mainly from secular theatrical sources; but while the musical techniques employed are largely those of the Italian Opera and Oratorio, the basic dramatic conception is much older in origin and stems from the ancient Passion-play tradition which had established a firm hold upon popular religious thought in Germany. The genius of Bach is however manifest in the perfect fusion of sacred and secular elements; in the great Passions, the composer gives full emphasis to the mystical church element without in any way sacrificing the humanity and artistic richness of the popular secular tradition. Viewed from an eighteenth-century perspective, medieval and renaissance Passion music appears to be music drama of premature birth. While it is clearly wrong to attempt to judge the artistic achievements of one age by the standards of another, we cannot help observing during the sixteenth century an apparent urge towards realistic drama which is constantly handicapped on the one hand by the impersonal style essential to church ritual, and on the other by the limitations of contemporary musical technique. This conflict between artistic ends and means is nowhere more clearly seen than in the musical settings of the crowd utterances.

The first step towards greater realism in the representation of the crowd was taken in the fifteenth century by the unknown composers who revitalized the ancient plainsong settings of the Passions with their choral versions of the *synagoga* part.[1] As we have noticed earlier, a limited degree of characterization was encouraged in the plainsong delivery of the Passion, but this was insufficient to create a realistic crowd effect; no amount of vocal expression ('*clamose et cum asperitate*') could make one man sound like a multitude. In the new Dramatic Passion form however a modicum of realism was immediately achieved by the contrast of the musical resources employed, the single line of the plainsong being set against the richer texture of the choral interruptions. Such a contrast was naturally less easily achieved in the sixteenth century Motet Passion form, where the individuality of the crowd became obscured in the wholly choral texture; but even here attempts were made to emphasize the crowd utterances by reducing the number of the voice-parts in the narrative passages immediately preceding them. It is nevertheless in the Dramatic Passion form that we must seek the

[1] It is important to remember that the traditional *synagoga* part included the utterances of all the minor characters as well as the crowd. A clear division, which reserved the choir entirely for the utterances of the crowd, did not occur until the late sixteenth century in the settings by Victoria.

seeds of later developments rather than in the musically more elaborate Motet type.

In the earlier part of the sixteenth century, the Catholic composers of Dramatic Passions adopted the current liturgical style of choral composition, virtually the motet style, for their settings of the crowd utterances. This style was extremely expressive, meditative, and well-suited for normal liturgical purposes, but quite undramatic; the texture of the music was usually wholly contrapuntal with imitative treatment of the vocal parts, and the words were frequently presented in an elaborately *melismatic* form, a single word or syllable being often set to a lengthy musical phrase. At this stage in the development of harmonic technique, dissonance, which was clearly a powerful means of dramatic expression, could only result from the free flow of the vocal parts in the contrapuntal texture; and then only under certain limited conditions. An expressive discord, such as the diminished seventh, had no separate existence outside its context in such a texture, and consequently such a dramatic effect as the single overwhelming shout of 'Barabbas', which occurs in Bach's St Matthew Passion, set to this very chord, would have been unimaginable. By skilful manipulation of the voices, a composer could occasionally make an expressive dissonance occur on a significant word such as 'betray' or 'crucify'; but this emotional style of word-painting was not a normal feature of the musical technique of this period. As an inevitable result of the conflict between the vocal parts which arose from the use of *melisma* and from this elaborate form of dissonance treatment, there was a considerable loss of clarity in the presentation of the text.

On the other hand, if we turn to the Lutheran composers of the same period we find that the clarity of the words was the primary consideration in the setting of the crowd choruses. All the expressive devices of the contemporary Roman ritual —*melisma*, contrapuntal imitation, and so on—were rejected in favour of the simplest possible type of chordal responses which followed the natural rhythm of the words. Indeed in some of the earliest examples of this type of Passion we frequently find a single chord used for an entire chorus and altered eventually only at the final cadence. Obviously, in this type of setting music has only the humblest of functions to fulfil; the most important consideration here is that the words should be clearly 'understanded of the people', a fundamental tenet of the Lutheran faith. In later examples of the Lutheran Dramatic Passion a similar simplicity of style prevails; in fact, so stereotyped are these short crowd responses, with their use of the transposed Ionian mode (akin to the modern F major) and mechanical cadence formulas, that it is astonishing to find that so many composers, even as late as the end of the seventeenth century, should have been impelled to compose them anew.

A compromise between the two extremes of style—intricate polyphony and simple declamation—is to be found in the Dramatic Passion settings by Catholic composers in the latter part of the sixteenth century, the period of the Counter-Reformation; these composers were, no doubt, encouraged to seek greater textual clarity by the recommendations of the Council of Trent (1545-63): '. . . the whole plan of singing in musical modes should be constituted not to give empty pleasure to the ear, but in such a way that the words may be clearly understood by all, and thus the hearts of the listeners may be drawn to the desire of heavenly harmonies.' In these settings of the crowd utterances, by a limitation of vocal *melisma* and of elaborate polyphonic imitation, the clarity of the words is preserved without recourse to the somewhat naïve chordal style of the contemporary German composers. These late-sixteenth-century Catholic composers, making a virtue out of a necessity, achieve a beautiful effect which suggests the pensive lamentation of a detached observer over past happenings rather than the life-like representation of present drama; this can be seen in the following example from the St John Passion (1585) by the Spanish composer Victoria:

Example 6   *St John Passion* (1585)   T. L. de Victoria

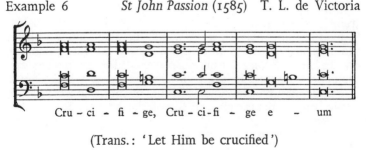

Cru – ci – fi – ge, Cru – ci-fi – ge e – um

(Trans.: 'Let Him be crucified')

'Very tame Jews, indeed', was the rather acid comment made by Mendelssohn on hearing a performance of this work nearly two hundred and fifty years after it was composed, possibly a not unnatural reaction from one who had studied the Bach Passion settings so closely, and who was so deeply imbued with the spirit of Lutheranism. Nevertheless it is clear that the Roman Catholic composers of the late sixteenth century, such as Victoria, Lassus and Byrd, were seeking, within the limitations of the current musical language and the natural sobriety imposed by the Roman ritual, the maximum immediacy of expression. There was at this period nothing colourless or unemotional in the Roman liturgy for Holy Week. Vivid detail would be presented to the congregation at the Stations of the Cross service; and in such related music as Palestrina's *Improperia* or Victoria's profound motet, *Tenebrae factae sunt*, there is an outstanding richness of emotional expression. As in the Lutheran Church, the human qualities of Christ and the actuality of the events of His life and death were deliberately stressed as being essential for the religious education of the people.

During the seventeenth century the crowd choruses in the German Oratorio Passions display for the most part a surprising conservatism. In the works by Thomas Selle, Christian Flor, and Johann Sebastiani, for example, we find the use of simple chordal responses akin to those of Johann Walter and other Lutheran composers of the previous century; these simple choruses are enlivened only by the addition of an instrumental accompaniment, which is confined almost entirely to doubling the vocal parts. There is disappointingly little evidence of the harmonic experiments which abound in other fields of composition; once again we see signs of the restraining influence which was continually exercised by the traditional ritualism of the Church. Only in Thomas Selle's St John Passion (1643), a work which reveals in many respects the influence of the great Venetian master, Giovanni Gabrieli, do we find chromaticism clearly used for expressive and dramatic purposes. In the following example, which should be compared with the Victoria setting of the same words given above, the chromatic movement of the bass (F, F sharp, G, G sharp, A) produces an effect of mounting excitement and fanaticism which foreshadows, in a simple form, one of Bach's characteristic pictorial devices. Despite the long note-values, the speed should be thought of as being very brisk.

Example 7   *St John Passion* (1643)   T. Selle

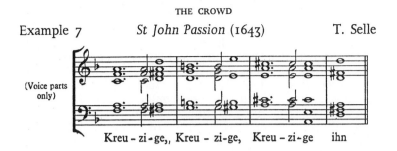

(Voice parts only)

Kreu – zi – ge,, Kreu – zi – ge, Kreu – zi – ge   ihn

The most effective seventeenth-century solution to the problem of realistic crowd representation is to be found in the liturgical Passions of Schütz. Schütz's choruses differ utterly from those of the typical German Dramatic Passions of the period; instead of a simple chordal technique, we find a vivid contrapuntal texture in which short, strongly rhythmic phrases are tossed in imitation between the various voices. There is practically no use of *melisma*, but by means of frequent word and phrase repetitions each chorus is formed into a movement of considerable length. The style here is clearly related to that of the late-sixteenth-century Italians,[1] though in numerous details of construction and expression Schütz displays a greatly superior sense of dramatic realism.

The revolutionary zeal of the Florentine innovators at the beginning of the seventeenth century had resulted in a temporary abandonment of counterpoint by progressive composers; but during the course of the century the ancient technique re-emerged in a new and modernized form and began to reveal a whole new range of expressive and dramatic possibilities. In his Passion settings, Schütz, as we have seen earlier, deliberately adopts the traditional dramatic method of presentation; but by means of such techniques as this new contrapuntal style he imparts to it a highly individual and original flavour. In the crowd choruses Schütz obtains perfect textual clarity by means of careful word accentuation and an almost complete rejection of *melisma*; but at the same time he achieves a remarkably life-like crowd effect by the use of short, well-defined rhythmic phrases which are combined in close contrapuntal imitation. Extra definition is given to these

[1] In fact, the vigour and expressive pictorialism of the writing has more in common with the secular madrigal style of the late renaissance period than with the strictly liturgical motet style.

vocal phrases by the frequent use of short rests inside the texture; these rests have the effect of focusing the listener's ear upon the individual voice-parts as they enter, and contribute much to the clarity and vitality of the presentation. It is however interesting to notice that the composer is careful to avoid rhetorical silences in all the voices simultaneously, and prefers to preserve continuity throughout each chorus in the sixteenth-century manner. By virtue of his contrapuntal style Schütz finds many opportunities for the expressive use of dissonance; he also gives several instances of simple but effective word-painting, such as the abrupt cries of '*Halt, halt*' in the chorus 'Wait, let's see whether Elias will come and save Him', from the St Matthew Passion, or the mocking laughter on the words '*lieber Juden König*' (dear King of the Jews) in the chorus of derisory homage from the St John Passion. In our next example, the opening of this chorus by Schütz is set side by side, for comparison, with a typical late-sixteenth-century setting of the same words (in Latin) by the Roman composer Francesco Soriano; notice how the mock solemnity of the opening of Schütz's chorus contrasts vividly with the rippling quavers which follow. (See Example 8 opposite.)

A further example of vivid realism occurs in the 'Crucify' chorus from Schütz's St John Passion where, by a sudden quickening of the tempo in the last four bars, the composer paints a graphic picture of an impatient crowd who are rapidly getting out of control.

An interesting problem arises in connection with a setting of St Mark's account which is frequently attributed to Schütz. This work appears, together with the other three Passions, in a beautifully-written copy which was made by Zacharias Gründig, a musician who was employed at the Dresden court at the end of the seventeenth century, shortly after the death of Schütz. Philip Spitta[1] has given convincing reasons for regarding the St Mark Passion as spurious, reasons which are based mainly on internal evidence. An examination of the work reveals that, while the narrative is written in a stiff, archaic plainsong style quite unlike the subtle declamation found in the St Matthew and St John Passions, the crowd choruses are set in a manner which, though superficially

---

[1] In the preface to vol. I of his edition (1885-94) of the complete works of Schütz. The St Mark Passion is reprinted in this volume.

Example 8   (a) *St John Passion* (1665)   H. Schütz
                  (b) *St John Passion* (*c.* 1590)   F. Soriano

(Trans.: Hail, (dear) King of the Jews)

similar to that of Schütz, really bears a much closer stylistic relationship to early-eighteenth-century music. The archaism of the narrative is in fact paralleled in Schütz's own early

67

Oratorio, the *Resurrection History* (1623), and also, to a lesser extent, in the St Luke Passion (1664); but such features in the choral writing as the absence of modal influence, the quasi-Handelian smoothness of the counterpoint, and the rhetorical breaks in the musical continuity, are all quite alien to the true Schütz style at any period of his career. Spitta tentatively suggests Johann Kuhnau, Bach's immediate predecessor at St Thomas's, Leipzig, as the possible author, though his motives for undertaking such a remarkable plagiarism remain obscure. Certainly Kuhnau shared Schütz's reactionary views about 'modernist' influences in Lutheran church music and he may have wished to demonstrate that the old style was not yet exhausted of expressive possibilities. Probably the question of authorship, as in the similar case of the spurious St Luke Passion attributed to Bach, will never now be finally resolved.

In Schütz's settings of the crowd scenes we find one of the earliest attempts to distinguish clearly between the various groups of people represented in the Gospel story. In the St Matthew Passion, by the use of many different combinations of high priests, scribes, elders, soldiers, Jews, disciples, and so on, he contrives to produce no less than thirteen distinct groups who are presented in the twenty crowd choruses. By no means all these combinations are in fact substantiated by the Gospel narrative. From the musical point of view only the broadest type of characterization is effective in the settings of the crowd choruses; this can be achieved either by changes of voice-colouring, as in Schütz's settings of the words of the high priests where the sopranos are omitted from the chorus, or by slight differences of musical style, as in the broad distinction which the composer creates between the disciple choruses and those of the hostile mob, the former being set in a less rhythmically energetic manner.

In St Matthew's account of the Passion, the disciples, as a group, have three important utterances which appear early in the narrative; the third of these, 'Lord, is it I?', which occurs immediately after the dramatic moment during the Last Supper when Christ horrifies His disciples with the words 'One of you shall betray Me', invariably receives special musical treatment. Clearly, music lacks the means of detailed individual characterization so wonderfully displayed in Leonardo da Vinci's famous picture 'The Last Supper' which portrays this very scene. In this masterpiece the painter vividly depicts the individual reactions of each of the disciples at this single moment; but, because of the limitations of the art, it is a static moment, frozen in time. Music however by its own special characteristics, is able to give life and movement to the scene, instead of merely suggesting it, and thus achieves a peculiar vividness of representation. In Bach's setting of this chorus, a short musical phrase, which contains the normal upward leap of the questioning voice, is tossed in imitation between the voices of the choir; later on in the chorus, the increasing anxiety and dismay of the questioners is subtly portrayed by the enlargement of the original upward leap of a fourth to one of a sixth, the interval which is also used by Judas in the succeeding recitative passage to represent his conscience-troubled question, 'Master, is it I?' This musical conception of the scene is by no means original; Bach is here, as so often, giving ideal expression to a traditional method of presentation which dates back to the early history of the Dramatic Passion form. Schütz's treatment of this chorus for instance is strikingly similar to Bach's with its use of closely overlapping imitations between the voice-parts. An earlier traditional method of setting this scene was to present the questioning phrases singly in each of the voices in turn, and end with the choir uniting in four-part harmony. This simple method of presentation, which naturally lacks the animation and realism which we find in Schütz and Bach, can be seen in the next example from the St Matthew Passion (1613) by Melchior Vulpius. (See Example 9 on following page.)

Sebastiani, in his St Matthew Passion of 1672, adopts this older procedure exactly; in his setting, the various voice-parts are marked to be sung 'solo', an idea which may very well have been traditional. Johann Theile, on the other hand, who was a pupil of Schütz, imitates his teacher's methods in this as in all his crowd choruses.[1]

From the time of Schütz, counterpoint plays an increasingly important part in the representation of the crowd. In Handel's St John Passion (1704), there are several interesting examples in the crowd choruses of the combination of contrapuntal and harmonic techniques. Particularly effective is the chorus 'Away with Him, crucify Him' in which the first section—a

---

[1] In the chorus 'Prophesy unto us', Theile actually borrows the main thematic idea from Schütz's own setting of these words.

vivid contrapuntal setting of the words 'Away with Him'—
ends with a dramatic silence followed by the words 'Crucify
Him' set to forceful block harmony; the contrapuntal section
then returns at a faster tempo, creating, as in the Schütz
setting mentioned above, a realistic picture of the growing
impatience and excitement of the crowd. This Passion has
particular interest as an example of a Handel Oratorio which
belongs primarily to the Teutonic musical tradition and

Example 9   *St Matthew Passion* (1613)   M. Vulpius

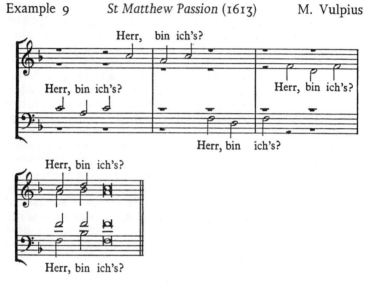

(Trans.: 'Lord, is it I?')

which was written before the composer came fully under the
influence of the Italian operatic and English choral styles; considering the youthfulness of the composer, the work displays
remarkable artistic unity and powers of dramatic characterization. Handel's second and last Passion composition, a setting
(dating from 1716) of the famous Passion poem *Der* . . .
gemarterte und sterbende Jesus by Heinrich Brockes, displays
a more polished technique and stronger affinities with the contemporary Italian operatic style, which the composer had no
doubt formed during his Italian visit (1706-09); but, largely
because of the muddled and inconsistent nature of the libretto,

the work forms a less convincing artistic whole than the earlier composition.

One important aspect of this inconsistency can be seen in the double use which Handel makes of the choir for dramatic and meditative purposes; in his setting of the Brockes libretto a confusion in the function of the choir arises from the close juxtaposition of choral settings of both crowd utterances and religious lyrical meditations. In all the seventeenth-century Passions which we have been considering, the only use of the choir for settings of non-Gospel words occurred in the opening and final choruses, and so, during the course of the actual Gospel narrative, the chorus was able to fulfil a quite unambiguous dramatic function.[1] But Handel's use of meditative choruses which are interpolated like arias and chorales into the narrative—a practice also employed to a limited extent by Bach—inevitably raises difficult aesthetic problems. In Bach's Passions, the choir is of course used to lead the singing of the congregation in the chorales which are interpolated into the Gospel narrative; but in this case, because of the distinctive style of the chorale melodies and the participation by the congregation, there is no danger of a confusion between the dramatic and meditative functions of the chorus. Similarly, in the case of the solo meditative arias which are accompanied by a chorale, ambiguity is avoided by the distinctive character of the accompanying melody. The most notable use of the choir for a setting of non-Gospel words is found in the chorus from the St Matthew Passion 'Have lightnings and thunders their fury forgotten?' Here, Bach shows great skill in blending his choral interpolation with the main body of the Gospel narrative. The movement opens with a reflective duet for soprano and alto 'Behold, my Saviour now is taken' which is punctuated by sharp, dramatic cries from the choir 'Loose Him! leave Him! bind Him not!', which, though not based on Gospel words, are set exactly in the style of a dramatic crowd chorus.[2] As the movement proceeds, the lyricism of the soloists is gradually submerged until

[1] The case of Thomas Selle's St John Passion (1643) is rather different; the choral *Intermedia* in this work are really interludes between the three main parts of the Passion and not direct interpolations into the middle of the narrative.

[2] A similar use of dramatic choral interjections does actually appear in Handel's Brockes Passion in the accompaniment to the soprano aria 'Haste ye souls': see p. 98.

71

the choir finally break out into their vehemently dramatic chorus. It should be noticed also that Bach is careful to place this chorus in a context (after the scene of the Agony at Gethsemane) where the Gospel account makes no provision for crowd utterances, and thus avoids a close juxtaposition of the two types of chorus.

In Bach's settings of the crowd utterances we find a remarkable vigour and aptness of characterization; these short choruses, which have no exact counterpart in any other musical form, reveal the wonderful technical skill and imagination of the composer. And yet, as is constantly apparent, Bach was no innovator; rather was he content to adopt the methods of the past and infuse into them a new and vital spirit. Certain features are new; for example, the linking together of the recitatives and the choruses and the use of inconclusive final cadences which produce a realistic effect of dramatic continuity; or again the vivid antiphonal writing for double chorus in the St Matthew Passion in which one choir echoes the shouts of the other. But the basic dramatic effects are achieved mainly by three simple musical techniques: the expressive use of chromaticism and dissonance; the contrapuntal interlacing of short, rhythmic vocal phrases; and the use of an independent orchestral accompaniment with its wide range of colourful pictorialism.

Bach's methods of employing these techniques can best be illustrated by reference to particular choruses in the Passions. Thus the realistic dramatic effect which is achieved by the use of chromaticism can be clearly seen in the chorus 'If this man were not a malefactor' from the St John Passion, where the rising movement of the bass (A, B flat, B natural, C, C sharp, D) vividly portrays the fanaticism of the crowd; this makes an interesting comparison with the chorus from Thomas Selle's St John Passion, given in example 7. (See Example 10 opposite; see also Appendix VIII, p. 154)

As an excellent example of Bach's use of counterpoint for the representation of the crowd there is the famous setting of 'Let Him be crucified' in the St Matthew Passion; in this chorus the voices enter in turn—from the bass upwards to the soprano —like the opening of a fugue, and present a strangely twisted theme which is characterized by syncopated rhythms and the sinister interval of the diminished fourth (G sharp to C). Here, the effect of the contrapuntal treatment, as in Schütz, is to

72

Example 10   *St John Passion* (1723)   J. S. Bach

give a life-like portrayal of the disjointed cries of the angry mob. At the opposite pole to this is the setting of the cry 'Barabbas' as a single unified shout. The traditional treatment of this scene was to make a short contrapuntal chorus out of this single word by repeating it five or six times. Bach has been criticized for a lack of realism in his setting; no un-disciplined crowd, say these critics, would shout with such unanimity. In fact, Bach's stroke of genius at this point transcends mere realism; in the words of Philip Spitta, the great biographer of Bach, the composer here 'depicts in the strongest manner the savage feeling of the populace by giving them a dramatic identity, and at the same time suggests the sudden horror which seizes the believing Christians at their answer'.[1] Finally, as a good illustration of Bach's masterly use of the orchestra for the accompaniment of the crowd choruses, let us turn again to the St John Passion. At the beginning of the work, the hostile crowd who have come to arrest Jesus reply twice to His question 'Whom seek ye?' with the words 'Jesus of Nazareth'; Bach accompanies these two short utterances with a swift, malicious musical figure played high up on the flutes and violins, which vividly emphasizes the malevolence of the crowd. This musical figure reappears three times later in the work as an accompaniment to the crowd choruses 'It is not lawful for us to put any man to death', 'Not this man, but Barabbas', and 'We have no king but Caesar', thereby acting as a *leit-motif* of hatred and envy and, incidentally, revealing a musical relationship between the choruses which is not otherwise immediately apparent.

Thus we find that Bach, building upon the techniques of the previous century, carries the realistic representation of the crowd to the furthest limits of theatricality; and yet, with extraordinary delicacy of judgment, he avoids overstepping the bounds of liturgical propriety. In these great Passions, the dramatic realism of the secular tradition and the ritual mysticism of the Church are clearly apparent as distinct constructive elements and are yet moulded together with sublime artistry.

[1] P. Spitta, *J. S. Bach* (translated by Clara Bell and J. A. Fuller-Maitland), Novello, 1951, Vol. 2, p. 546. (pub. in U.S.A. by Dover)

VI

THE LYRICAL ELEMENT:
(1) CHORALES

UNLIKE his fellow reformers Zwingli and Calvin, who
adopted a definitely hostile attitude towards music, Luther
valued the art highly as a servant of religion. Numerous
extracts from his writings testify to the extent of his admira-
tion and to the excellence of his taste. In a letter to the composer Ludwig Senfl, dated October 4th, 1530, he writes, 'I
am not ashamed to confess publicly that next to theology
there is no art which is the equal of music', and goes on to
state his belief that the devil 'flees from the voice of music
just as he flees from the words of theology'. In another place
he writes, 'I have always loved music. Those who have
mastered this art are made of good stuff, they are fit for any
task'.

Luther realized how strong an influence music could be in
furthering his cherished cause of greater congregational participation in the church services; while the use of the German
language would increase lay understanding, the singing of
hymns and psalms would give the whole body of worshippers
a central function in the liturgy. In the new church the inter-
mediary rôle of the priesthood was to be limited and greater
emphasis was to be placed upon the conception of Jesus Christ
as the 'only mediator and advocate' between the worshipper
and God. Thus the provision of suitable congregational music,
whereby the people could give direct expression to their
religious emotions, was regarded by Luther as an important
factor in the reconstruction of the liturgy.

For such a purpose the music had of necessity to be simple,
broad in style and easily memorable. Elaborate melodic or
rhythmic patterns were clearly unsuitable for a large body of
unskilled singers and, in view of the strophic nature of the
hymns, the tunes had to be capable of fitting the various verses

without undue attention to expressive or pictorial details. Thanks however to the liberality of Luther's views, composers were not expected to confine themselves to writing music of a purely congregational type and there was a parallel development of a more complex style of church composition. Congregational hymns nevertheless continually exercised a controlling function over the Lutheran church services and ensured a universality of devotional expression which is in marked contrast to the mystical remoteness and elaboration which characterizes much of the contemporary music for the Roman ritual. At a later stage in the history of the Lutheran Church, chorale melodies fulfilled a similar function to the plainsong melodies of the Catholic Church in their use as central themes (*cantus firmi*) around which elaborate compositions were built.

Luther himself was one of the chief pioneers in the provision of suitable songs for the people to sing. In the *Formulae Missae et Communionis* of 1523 he writes 'I desire also that we have more songs in the vernacular of the people', and in the following year in the preface to the *Geistliches Gesangbüchlein* (The little book of spiritual songs) he writes 'I, together with several others, have collected a number of spiritual songs in order that a beginning might be made to prepare and gather such material and also that others, whose ability is greater than ours, be induced to do such work.' For the verses of these first chorales Luther and his assistants drew entirely from older material, adapting and borrowing from pre-Reformation German hymns and secular folk songs or translating and remodelling some of the Latin songs of the Catholic Church.

Throughout the Middle Ages the Church in Germany had maintained a vigorous tradition of hymn-singing. This semi-liturgical, semi-popular art had survived largely because of the comparative remoteness of Germany from direct papal control and, though typically medieval in its strange mixture of superstition and ill-digested dogma, was to prove a most valuable source of hymns for the new Church. Some outstanding examples of these songs have survived to the present day; a characteristic instance, with its mixture of Latin and German words, is the Christmas hymn *In dulci jubilo, Nun singet und seid froh*.

Direct translations from the Latin resulted in such German

paraphrases as *Komm, Heiliger Geist, Herre Gott* (Come, Holy Ghost, Lord God) which was adapted by Luther from the *Veni Sancte Spiritus*, or the *Christe du Lamm Gottes*, taken from the simple form of the *Agnus Dei*. From these varied sources, the early Protestant writers began to design a body of hymns which were to express 'a spontaneous outburst of love and reverence for God'. By the time of Luther's death in 1546 more than sixty collections of chorales had been published. These hymns rapidly gained widespread popularity and certainly contributed as much to the spread of the Reformer's doctrines as his writings and sermons.

The work of finding suitable melodies for the new hymns was entrusted mainly to Luther's personal advisers, Johann Walter and Conrad Rupff, who were both in turn directors of the court choir at Dresden. As with the hymn verses, the majority of the early chorale melodies were borrowed and adapted from earlier sources, mainly from Latin hymnody and German secular folk-song. Some of the most solemn Protestant hymns are associated with melodies of startlingly secular origins. A good example is the chorale *Was mein Gott will* (O Father let Thy will be done) which is used by Bach in the St Matthew Passion during the scene in the Garden at Gethsemane. The melody of this chorale was derived originally from a French love-song entitled *Il me suffit de tous mes maux*, which was published in Paris in 1529. Similarly, the melody of *O Haupt voll Blut und Wunden* (O Sacred Head) originated as a popular German song *Mein G'müt ist mir verwirret* (My heart is troubled) by Hans Leo Hassler, dating from 1601.

At the earliest stage the tunes were not harmonized and, in the characteristic manner of the period, were extremely free rhythmically. Later, florid contrapuntal parts were added while the melody was kept in the tenor voice-part. Eventually the melody rose to the surface of the music, the lower parts provided a simple harmonic support and, in a gradual process of development which lasted through the seventeenth century, the madrigal-like rhythmic freedom gave way to the strictly metrical versions which are familiar from the settings of Bach. In the following example a comparison of the versions by Hassler and Bach of the famous Passion chorale melody 'O Sacred Head surrounded' shows clearly the change in rhythmic structure.

Example 11

    (a) 'O Sacred Head'—version by H. L. Hassler (1601)
    (b) 'O Sacred Head'—version by J. S. Bach (1729)

(a)
(original
note-values
halved)

(b)

At the end of the sixteenth century, the creative period of the chorale began and many German poets began to make original contributions to the growing corpus of Lutheran hymns. The most notable of these earlier writers was Johann Heermann (1585-1647), the author of *Herzliebster Jesu, was hast du verbrochen* (O blessed Jesu, how hast Thou offended), three verses of which appear in Bach's St Matthew Passion. The succeeding generation of Protestant writers included such outstanding men as Johann Rist (1607-67), Paul Gerhardt (1607-76), and Johann Franck (1618-77). Paul Gerhardt, the author of *O Haupt voll Blut und Wunden*, was undoubtedly the greatest of the Protestant lyric poets; at the height of his fame he became associated with Pietists, to whose subjective aspirations he gave perfect lyrical expression. The Pietist movement, however, despite its association with this remarkable poet, exercised generally a weakening influence on the structure of the chorale by its emphasis on personal religious emotion at the expense of the universality which had been typical of the finest chorales since the earliest Reformation times. The classic example of the Pietist hymn-book was the one published in the early eighteenth century by J. A. Freylinghausen at Halle, the principal centre of Pietism; this work contained some seven hundred hymns by a host of eminent poets and musicians. The poetry of this creative period of the chorale was matched in excellence by the melodies of such composers as Johann Schop (d. *c.* 1665), Melchior Franck (d. 1639), and Johann Crüger (1598-1662), the author of the great melody which appears three times in the St Matthew Passion set to verses of Heermann's hymn *Herzliebster Jesu*.

From the earliest days of the Lutheran Church, the simple but memorable chorale melodies became firmly associated with particular aspects of religious thought and ritual and thus acted as a powerful factor in the religious education of the people. By the time of Bach, the process of assimilation had so developed that a church composer could be reasonably certain that by the introduction of a popular chorale melody into a cantata or organ prelude he could bring a significant religious idea into focus in the worshippers' minds; a process not unlike that of the *leit-motif* in Wagnerian music drama. So strong was the power of musical association that even the audibility of the words (frequently very slight in a complicated polyphonic composition) was of little account; the mere sound of the well-known melody was sufficient stimulus. Even to-day, for many people, the sound of the great Passion hymn ' O Sacred Head surrounded ' evokes more powerfully than any other feature in Bach's Passion music the mood of the mystery of Passiontide.

A chorale melody might appear in the musical portions of the Lutheran services in many forms; as an elaborately-decorated melody in an organ prelude or fantasia (thus making the ' Voluntary ' an integral part of the service); as a *cantus firmus* in a complicated polyphonic chorus from a cantata, motet or Passion; or as a simple setting of a congregational hymn in which the significance of the words was often under-lined by expressive harmonies. In this way the chorale became one of the most important structural features of Lutheran church music.

It was not until quite late in the seventeenth century that simple congregational settings of chorales began to appear printed in the scores of Passion Oratorios. It seems fairly certain however that in accordance with the demands of local custom chorales were sung at Passion performances considerably earlier, though there is little direct evidence of this. One indication is given in a St Matthew Passion by Thomas Mancinus, dating from 1637, in which there are cues interspersed throughout the score which show where chorales and *symphonias* may be performed. In all probability these cues were added some time after the original date of composition, but they may well indicate the normal places where chorale and instrumental interpolations were made in performances of the traditional Dramatic Passions. Certainly a substantial number of chorales were written which were directly connected with the Passion story and it is difficult to believe that these were not introduced during the singing of the Passion. The later seventeenth-century Passions seem to indicate an established custom whereby the chorale *O Traurigkeit, O Herzeleid* (O Grief, O Suffering) by Johann Rist was sung at the end of the Passion story, and the constant appearance of the hymn *O Lamm Gottes unschuldig*, a translation of the *Agnus Dei* by Nicholas Decius, suggests that it too was a firm favourite. The most notable of all these Passion chorales is Paul Stockmann's *Jesu, Leiden, Pein und Tod* (Jesu, suffering pain and death) which presents the complete Passion story in a microcosm; Bach uses three verses of this hymn in the St John Passion.

Let us turn at once to the Passions of Bach, observe the function of the congregational chorales and attempt to relate Bach's practice to that of earlier composers. In the St Matthew Passion there are twelve chorale verses for the congregation and six melodies are used, the famous Passion chorale melody appearing five times at focal points during the narrative. The St John Passion on the other hand contains eleven verses with eight different melodies. A direct comparison of the placing of the chorales in these two works is difficult because of the great differences in dramatic construction which we have noticed earlier, but the underlying policy is quite clear in both cases. Significant moments in the story are made the subject of comment and meditation by the assembled worshippers and chorale verses are chosen for the appropriateness of the sentiments which they express. The following examples show clearly the way in which Bach places his chorales in apt relationship to the narrative.

In the St Matthew Passion: (a) After Jesus has revealed to His disciples that one of them is to betray Him, they ask anxiously, 'Lord, is it I?' The chorale which follows gives a direct answer to this question in a personal acknowledgment of sin by the whole congregation. ''Tis I whose sin now binds Thee, with anguish deep surrounds Thee, and nails Thee to the Tree.' (b) After the scene of the death of Christ, the believers reflect upon their own mortality in the chorale 'Be near me, Lord, when dying, O part not Thou from me!'

In the St John Passion: After Jesus's words 'but if I have spoken well, why smitest thou Me?', the congregation express horror in the words ' O Lord, who dares to smite Thee? ' Clearly Bach is following Luther's precepts in giving the congregation a central function in the presentation of the Passion and in ensuring that each stage in the unfolding of the story is carefully followed and understood. Modern performances of the Passions in which the chorales are left to be sung unaccompanied by the choir go directly against Bach's musical and liturgical intentions; the chorales are clearly marked to receive full orchestral accompaniment and the function of the choir at these places is to lead the singing of the congregation. In this connection it is of course necessary to realize the changed conditions under which the Passions are usually performed nowadays. In place of liturgical performances in church before a devout congregation steeped in the appropriate musical and religious traditions, we now frequently have concert performances which may take place in a theatre or hall with no sacred associations and before an audience who are probably little in sympathy with the tenets of the Lutheran faith.

The earliest surviving Passion which includes simple chorales printed in the score is a setting by Johann Sebastiani of St Matthew's account, dating from 1672. Sebastiani, who was born at Weimar in 1622 and later lived and worked at Königsberg, introduces thirteen chorale verses into his work and these are set to eight different melodies. In every case the setting given in the score is for a solo voice with an accompaniment for viols and *continuo*. This would seem to imply that these chorales were intended for performance as vocal arias, but the existence of a booklet on the performance of Passion music, which was published at Königsberg in 1682, sheds more light on the matter. This booklet, which was expressly designed for the guidance of congregations, indicates clearly that at certain points a solo voice is to sing and at others the whole congregation.

Nevertheless in view of the probability of an ancient tradition of purely congregational singing at Passion performances, mentioned above, these first appearances of chorale settings in the score seem to be symptomatic of the growing tendency for congregations to leave the expression of reflective commentary to a trained solo singer. It was partly from such solo versions of the chorales that there evolved the independent meditative arias which became increasingly important in Passion compositions in the last quarter of the seventeenth century. An early anticipation of this occurs in the St Matthew Passion (1667) by Christian Flor, in which twelve interpolated chorale verses are set as solo arias to freely-composed music; this music contains only occasional fragments from the associated chorale melodies and was certainly not intended for congregational performance. Such arias of course fulfil a similar function to the chorales by providing lyrical commentary on the development of the story, but do not involve active participation by the congregation. They will be reserved for fuller discussion in the next chapter. An even clearer distinction between the two types of lyrical meditation is to be found in the St Matthew Passion (1700) by J. G. Kühnhausen in which, of the ten chorale verses, five are set as congregational hymns and the remainder as soprano solos or duets.

In all these works the method of placing the chorales in direct relationship to the incidents of the drama is exactly similar to Bach's. For example, in Sebastiani and Flor the scene of Peter's denial of Christ is followed by the chorale *Erbarm' dich mein, O Herre Gott* (Have mercy upon me, O Lord God), while in Kühnhausen, it is followed by *Mein' Sünden mich zwar kranken sehr* (My sins are very grievous to me). In both cases the congregation transfer to themselves Peter's sin of faithlessness. The chorale verse which follows this scene in Bach's St John Passion is taken from Paul Stockmann's hymn *Jesu, Leiden, Pein und Tod*:

> 'Peter in forgetfulness, thrice denied his Master,
> One look moved him to confess, weeping, his disaster.
> Jesus, turn to look on me, who persist in sinning,
> Set my fettered conscience free, free for new beginning'

The reference in this verse to 'one look' recalls the imaginative touch in St Luke's narrative where, after the account of Peter's denial and the crowing of the cock, the Evangelist writes 'And the Lord turned and looked on Peter'.[1] The same scene in Bach's St Matthew Passion is selected for special treat-

[1] It is interesting to notice the use of a similar idea in Sebastiani's setting of this scene; the narrator sings 'And Peter remembered the words of Jesus, which said unto him' and, at this point, the *actual* voice of Jesus takes up the 'remembered' words 'before the cock

ment. Lyrical commentary is provided by both an aria
Erbarme dich, mein Gott (Have mercy, Lord, on me), and by
a congregational chorale *Bin ich gleich von dir gewichen*
(Lamb of God, I fall before Thee), which offers hope of comfort and forgiveness to the repenting sinner.

An interesting use of the chorale for more strikingly
dramatic purposes occurs, both in Flor and Sebastiani, after
the crowd's venomous shout, 'He is guilty of death'. Here the
word *schuldig* (guilty) brings an immediate response from the
congregation in the first line of the succeeding chorale, *O
Lamm Gottes* un*schuldig* (O guilt*less* Lamb of God). At this
point the congregation, with their emphatic denial of the
words of accusation, seem to abandon their normal rôle as
detached commentators and enter directly into the framework
of the drama. This same dramatic device also occurs in the
St Matthew Passion by Johann Meder which was composed at
Danzig about the year 1700. There are only five chorales in
this Passion; four verses of *O Lamm Gottes* placed at separate
points in the narrative and an elaborate setting[1] of *O Traurigkeit, O Herzeleid*, placed (as also in Flor, Sebastiani and Kühnhausen) in its traditional place at the end of the narrative. In
the original manuscript some of the chorales, arias and duets
are pasted into the score and are presumably later additions;
the handwriting is the same as that used in the rest of the
score, though the ink appears to be different. The implication
is that these additions were made by Meder or his copyist for
a particular performance at which a fairly extensive use of
lyrical interpolations was to be permitted. (See App. VII, p. 147)

A notable characteristic of Bach's chorale settings which dis-
tinguishes them from those of his predecessors lies in the
frequent use made of expressive harmonic colouring to emphasize particular words or the meaning of particular phrases.
As in the harmonic accompaniment which supports the

crow twice, thou shalt deny Me thrice'. It is pleasant to suppose that
Sebastiani was here supplying a touch of poetic fancy akin to that
in St Luke's Gospel, though it is of course possible that this was simply
a slip on the part of the composer.
[1] The five verses are set as follows:
    1. Soprano solo with 2 violette and *continuo*
    2. Tenor solo with 2 oboes and *continuo*
    3. Chorus (S.A.T.B.) with oboes and *continuo*
    4. Solo soprano, tenor, and bass with ornate accompaniment
    5. Full setting for chorus, orchestra and *continuo*

vocal recitatives, chromatic and dissonant chords are often used to paint such words as 'death', 'fear', 'pain', 'sorrow'. That such a symbolical use of harmony to interpret the meaning of the text was a life-long feature of Bach's style can be seen from a report of the consistory at Arnstadt where Bach was organist from 1703-1707, in which the composer is reproved for 'having hitherto made many curious *variationes* in the chorale, and mingled many strange tones in it, and for the fact that the congregation has been confused by it.' The confusion of the congregation, when their ears were assailed by such a chord as that which accompanies the word 'death'[1] in the following example, can be readily imagined. Beautiful though the harmonic effect is here, it is worth noticing that the grimness of the chord is in fact curiously at variance with the meaning of the whole phrase, which tells rather of hope and comfort.

Example 12   *St John Passion* (1723)   J. S. Bach

Death shall   come with – out   dis – tress

In view of the importance of the part played by the chorale in the music of Bach, it is surprising to find that Heinrich Schütz, his greatest predecessor, makes practically no use of the great hymn melodies. Chorale verses are adopted for the final choruses of all his Passion compositions, but in only one instance is any use made of the traditional melodies. This occurs at the end of the St John Passion where, in a motet setting of the eighth verse of the Passiontide hymn *Christus der uns selig macht* (Christ, that makes us blessed) by Michael Weisse, the soprano part is a paraphrase of the tune *Patris*

[1] The original German of this passage reads *Stirb daraus ohn' alles Leid* (*Die* henceforth without distress).

Sapientia,[1] which first appeared with the words in 1531, the original date of publication. The connection between the ancient melody and Schütz's voice-part can be seen in the following example:

Example 13   (a) CHORALE MELODY: *Patris Sapientia* (1531)
              (b) *St John Passion* (1665)   H. Schütz

In the other liturgical Passions and in the short Oratorio, *The Seven Last Words from the Cross,* Schütz sets chorale texts to freely-composed music in motet style. Outstanding amongst these is the final chorus of the St Matthew Passion which uses the last verse of the chorale *Ach, wir armen Sünder* (Ah, we poor sinners) by Hermann Bonn, and ends most beautifully with an expressive setting of the *Kyrie Eleison.*

It must be remembered that, though Schütz was a German composer writing for the Lutheran Church, much of his technique of composition was learned with Italian masters. The idea of introducing popular art, such as the Lutheran chorale, into finished and perfected compositions was no doubt alien to the spirit of a composer who was so deeply imbued with the aristocratic traditions of the Italian Renaissance. It needed the greatness of Bach to achieve a perfect fusion between popular and aristocratic elements and then only by

[1] A 'modernized' version of this melody was used twice by Bach in the St John Passion at the beginning of the second part of the work and after the account of the piercing of Christ's side by the soldiers.

means of musical techniques which were far beyond the range of Schütz.

This perfect fusion is nowhere better demonstrated than in the great choruses in the Bach Passions which are based on chorale melodies woven into the texture. The St Matthew Passion contains three notable examples: (i) the opening chorus 'Come ye daughters, share my mourning', in which the chorale *O Lamm Gottes unschuldig*, sung by trebles, floats serenely over the complicated choral texture of the double choir; (ii) the meditative chorus during the Agony in the Garden at Gethsemane, 'O grief! that bows the Saviour's troubled heart'; and (iii) the wonderful chorale fantasia 'O man, thy grievous sin bemoan', which ends the first part of the Passion and which stood originally as the opening chorus of the St John Passion. In its revised form, without this incomparable fantasia movement, the St John Passion contains only one of these chorale choruses, 'My Lord and Saviour, let me ask Thee', which follows the scene of the death of Christ. In this movement the bass soloist questions the dead Saviour about the promise of eternal life, while the chorus in the background quietly sing a verse of Stockmann's hymn, *Jesu, Leiden, Pein und Tod*. This combination of a solo voice with the chorus, a favourite device of Bach's, is even more effectively used in the St Matthew chorus, 'O grief! that bows the Saviour's troubled heart!' in which the anguished phrases of the tenor soloist are interspersed with single lines of the third verse of Heermann's hymn *Herzliebster Jesu* set to Johann Crüger's great melody. The movement is a study in vivid contrasts blended paradoxically into a perfect unity. The high angular vocal line of the tenor soloist contrasts with the low pitch and smooth outline of the chorale; the expressive woodwind and strings accompaniment of the tenor contrasts with the simple organ accompaniment of the chorale; and yet, from the very sharpness of these contrasts, Bach achieves an ideal blend of personal and universal religious expression. Spitta has drawn attention to the wonderfully vivid effect which must have been achieved in this aria by Bach's placing of the two choirs on either side of the organ gallery in St Thomas's church, an effect which is inevitably lost in modern performances with soloists who are independent of the two choirs. 'When, in the scene on the Mount of Olives, one voice in the first choir sings "O grief! Now pants His agonizing heart" and from the other side the chorale rises up like the penitential prayer of a kneeling congregation, "O Saviour, why must all this ill befall Thee?" the effect must have bordered closely on the dramatic.'[1] In the score Bach emphasizes the solemn character of this chorale by specifically directing the choir to sing softly throughout.

In the original version of the St Matthew Passion the first part ended with a simple congregational chorale, *Jesum lass ich nicht von mir* (Jesus, I hold fast to Thee); many years later, at the end of his life, the composer substituted for this chorale the great chorus *O Mensch bewein' dein' Sünde gross* (O man, thy grievous sin bemoan) which stood originally as the opening chorus of the St John Passion. Traces can be found of the original rôle of this chorus as an introduction to the Passion story. The words 'until the appointed time drew nigh, when He should be betrayed and slain' are not strictly appropriate in their present context halfway through the narrative; but the musical gain which results from the transfer far outweighs such considerations. In this great movement the famous melody by Matthäus Greitter (1525) is sung by the sopranos, each line separately, while the lower parts add expressive contrapuntal patterns in quavers. To complete the texture the orchestra (flute and oboe tone predominating) accompanies with continuous semi-quavers slurred together in pairs, a favourite *motif* with Bach for the expression of grief. The whole movement forms one of the great corner-stones of the Passion and a wholly satisfying end to the first part. There is no better example of the sublime art by which Bach could transform a simple hymn into a massive and elaborate choral composition.

Bach is unique for his time in the use which he makes of chorales. His great contemporaries Handel, Keiser, Telemann and Mattheson tended to regard the ancient hymns as an outmoded form of expression in church music, which had no place in the new, elegant, more theatrical style. But in the Passions and the later church cantatas and organ works, Bach repeatedly affirms the importance of the chorales as a vital source of religious and musical inspiration and thereby retains a valuable link with the true Lutheran tradition.

[1] P. Spitta, *J. S. Bach* (Trans. by Clara Bell and J. A. Fuller-Maitland), Vol. 2, p. 540. (pub. in U.S.A. by Dover)

VII

THE LYRICAL ELEMENT:
(2) ARIAS AND CHORUSES

ONE of the major problems in operatic composition is presented by an inherent conflict between dramatic and lyrical elements. Opera is an attempt to reconcile two arts—music and drama—which are, by nature, fundamentally opposed. The essence of drama lies in continuity and development, in the growth of one situation from another, and in the revelation of unsuspected facets in events and personalities. Music on the other hand has natural lyrical and reflective characteristics which are essentially static and decorative and cannot adapt themselves to the speed of dramatic development. In order to keep pace with drama, music has to subordinate itself and sacrifice many of its fundamental lyrical qualities. Thus a reconciliation can only be achieved by a compromise which modifies considerably the basic attributes of both arts. The path of operatic history is strewn with discarded conventions which have served their turn in the attempt to resolve this basic conflict.

In a simple form, the conflict was present in the experimental music dramas of the early Florentine monodists. The *stile rappresentativo* was, as we have seen in an earlier chapter, designed primarily as a simple method of presenting dramatic speech in song; in this style the function of the music was entirely subordinate to that of the drama. But even here, despite the rigidness of the underlying artistic theories, the lyrical element in music began to assert itself at the expense of pure drama, and short sections of more highly organized melody began to appear among the wastes of simple dramatic declamation. As the Opera form developed, this distinction between the dramatic and lyrical elements became more sharply defined and gave rise to two distinct musical techniques which form the basis of all operatic conventions; recitative—the musical vehicle for dramatic and narrative speech, and aria—the melodic song which, though detrimental to dramatic development, provides the musical interest and variety essential to this hybrid art-form.

When we turn to the German Oratorio Passions of the seventeenth century we find similar attempts to achieve a balance between dramatic and lyrical elements. The main musical techniques employed in Oratorio were, as we have seen earlier, virtually identical to those used in Opera—recitatives, arias, instrumental interludes, and choruses. It was of course a primary concern of the Oratorio librettist to construct his text in such a way that it would afford good opportunities to the composer for a balanced and varied use of these techniques. But in the case of Passion music the 'libretto' was the original Gospel account; and though this made ample provision for the use of dramatic techniques such as recitative and chorus, it offered no scope for the employment of purely lyrical music. Thus if Passion composers were to achieve the same balance between dramatic and lyrical elements as had become normal in works written for the stage, poetic texts had inevitably to be added to the basic Gospel account.

The interpolation of lyrical texts into Passion music was an innovation of considerable moment. For centuries the hallowed words of the Gospels had been presented practically unaltered at Passiontide. The compilers of the early Motet Passion texts had indeed taken some liberties with the various accounts by omitting verses and by combining different sections to form a composite version; but none had dared to insert original verses of his own composition. In the last chapter we observed how the congregational chorale was gradually accepted into Passion settings, and fulfilled a liturgical function by focusing the worshippers' minds on significant stages in the unfolding of the drama. These congregational hymns, which were composed in an austere church style and which had been fathered by Luther himself, had the stamp of respectability; the interpolation of these as lyrical relief clearly involved little violation of the traditions of the Church. But the sacred aria which began to take the place of the congregational chorale as the seventeenth century progressed, was, with its secular theatrical associations, far less readily acceptable.

The first Passion to include in the score solo vocal arias, as opposed to simple congregational chorales, was Christian

Flor's setting of St Matthew which was composed in 1667. In this work we find the first signs of a recognizable system in the placing of the lyrical interpolations in relation to the Gospel text and in the distribution of the various musical forms—aria, instrumental *symphonia* and motet. In all there are nine vocal arias, involving soprano, alto, tenor and bass soloists, eleven short instrumental pieces and two motets for a five-part choir; the instrumental *symphonias* are, as we have seen before, used mainly to break up the lengthy scene of the Agony in the Garden. For the texts of his arias, Flor relies chiefly on chorale verses, though he also includes a few original stanzas by his poet friend Johann Rist[1]; and in the majority of cases, the arias are set in the style of chorale paraphrases and thus retain a link with church tradition. In the example which follows, the opening of one of Flor's arias is set beside the first line of the ancient chorale melody which it paraphrases; the words of the aria, *Christe, du Lamm Gottes*, are a translation of the *Agnus Dei*, which first appeared in 1557, associated with this chorale melody:

Example 14
   (a) CHORALE MELODY: *Christe, du Lamm Gottes* (1557)
   (b) *St Matthew Passion* (1667)   C. Flor

[1] Johann Rist (1607-67), poet and musician, was the founder of a song-school in Hamburg and the author of numerous sacred and secular poems.

It will be noticed that the fourth and fifth bars of the aria reproduce exactly the notes of the first phrase of the chorale; later phrases in the chorale are similarly paraphrased in the continuation of the aria. Other well-known chorale melodies such as *O Lamm Gottes unschuldig* and *O Traurigkeit, O Herzeleid* are also used in this way by Flor as a basis for his arias.

In the placing of his lyrical interpolations in relation to the Gospel text Flor adopts a scheme which, in its general principles, appears to have been followed by later composers right up to Bach. We find, for example, that after the scene of Peter's denial the composer introduces his only soprano aria— a setting of the words *Erbarm' dich mein* (Have mercy on me), and that this corresponds very closely to Bach's treatment of this scene in the St Matthew Passion where there is, in fact, an alto aria based on similar words *Erbarme dich, mein Gott* (Have mercy, Lord, on me). It seems quite possible that Bach may have come into contact with Flor's work when he visited Lüneburg in the year 1700. When Flor died in 1697, he was succeeded as organist at the church of St Lambert and St John by his son, Johann Georg, who undoubtedly preserved his father's musical traditions. It is, however, difficult to give any direct evidence of Bach's knowledge of this, or indeed of the majority of the earlier Passions. One can only draw attention to the clear continuity of the religious and musical tradition which, through generations of North German musicians, must eventually have influenced the thought of Bach.

After the scene of the death of Jesus, Flor inserts a five-part motet based on the words *Ecce quomodo moritur justus* (Behold, how the righteous Man dies), which provides an interesting example of the mixture of old and new styles and of the combination of Latin and German texts within the same work. There is strong evidence to suggest that it was customary in Passion performances to sing at this point the famous setting of these words by the Slavonic composer Jacobus Gallus (1550-91), but in this case the composition is by Flor himself. This most solemn moment in the Gospel story is selected for particularly rich meditative treatment in Flor's Passion; in addition to the motet, which has two halves separated by an instrumental *symphonia*, there is an alto aria *Ist dieser nicht des Höchsten Sohn?* (Is not this the Son of the Highest?), preceded by an extended instrumental introduction. The choice of the emotionally-coloured alto voice for this moment of pathos is fully in keeping with the normal practice of the Baroque period. Flor's work is remarkable for its lavishness in the use of meditative interpolations. In few of the later Oratorio Passions before Bach is there such a comprehensive scheme for lyrical commentary on the various events in the Gospel story. (See Appendix VI, p. 143)

In the St Matthew Passion (1673) by the Lübeck composer Johann Theile, there are only five arias: three for soprano, one for tenor, and one, a final movement in the form of a hymn of thanks, for five-part chorus and orchestra. These arias differ from those of Flor in their complete avoidance of chorale melodies and in their greater intricacy of musical construction. Though musically quite simple, the songs display a degree of sensitivity and formal organization which is far in advance of the primitive paraphrase technique of Flor, and which is reminiscent in many ways of the art of such notable song-writers of the period as Heinrich Albert (1604-51), a nephew of Schütz, and Adam Krieger (1634-66). In each case, the various verses of the arias are divided by short orchestral sections in which, very often, the aria melody is elaborated by contrapuntal imitations. Theile follows Flor's example in placing his arias at focal points in the narrative: after the Institution of the Holy Communion, after the crowd chorus ' Prophesy to us, Christ, who is it that struck Thee? ' after the scene of Peter's denial, after the words '. . . and led Him out to crucify Him', and at the end of the whole work. In two later settings of St Matthew's account by Johann Kühnhausen and Johann Meder, which date from the year 1700, a similar scheme is used in the placing of the interpolations, though here both congregational chorales and sacred arias are used to supply the meditative commentary. Meder's Passion contains an interesting aria based on the words *Christe du Lamm Gottes*; the setting is for a solo soprano with accompaniment for recorder, viols and *continuo*, and as in Flor's version of the same words, the familiar chorale melody is used as the basis of a chorale paraphrase. The melody is divided into three short vocal phrases, the last bar of which, in each case, is immediately echoed by the recorder with a remarkably expressive effect. In Flor's setting of this aria the orchestral parts which provide the accompaniment are lost; but an examination of the harmonies indicated by the figured bass reveals that a similar echo effect was quite possibly intended.

And so we witness during the second half of the seventeenth century the gradual growth of a new and important element in Passion music; from this point in the development of the form increasing emphasis was laid on the function of reflective commentary in the presentation of the drama. Under the influence of new aesthetic and religious principles, the purely objective style of the old Dramatic type of Passion was rapidly discredited and gave place to a more emotional and rhetorical manner of presentation in which devotional meditations about the Passion were considered more important than the direct and realistic enactment of the story. And increasingly, as the new musical styles of the Opera house began to permeate the services of the Church, congregations were content to leave the expression of this rhetorical reflection to trained solo singers and choirs. The austere musical and poetic style of the ancient church hymns gradually fell into disfavour, and the demand for a more elaborate form of vocal music was paralleled by a desire for a more subjective and emotional type of religious verse.

These developments in Lutheran Germany reflect, in a milder form, the new relationship between music and the church liturgy which had arisen in Catholic countries, notably Italy, during the seventeenth century. Guided by the spirit of the Counter-Reformation and by the new artistic ideals of the age, many Catholic church musicians had repudiated the liturgical techniques of the late Renaissance—those of Palestrina and his contemporaries—and had endeavoured to increase the range and appeal of their music by borrowing from secular stylistic sources. In Italy the influence of the rapidly developing Opera soon became apparent in church music. The pure polyphonic styles of the past no longer satisfied a public who were forming new musical tastes in the Opera theatre; as congregations in church, this public expected to find a richness of musical style similar to that which delighted them in the theatre. The epitome of this style was the Italian operatic aria; because of the sensuous nature of its melody and the dazzling brilliance of its bravura, the aria made a powerful emotional appeal which was found to be as effective for sacred as for secular purposes. A few more sensitive musicians, recognizing the dangers of excessive secularization, attempted to revive the older church traditions and composed polyphonic Masses and motets in a style akin to that of Palestrina; but the majority were content to yield to the demands of popular taste and provide church music in an ever more brilliant operatic manner. The elaborate nature of the Catholic ritual lent itself admirably to the purposes of histrionic display; and inevitably the rôle of Italian congregations changed increasingly from that of devout worshippers to that of passive spectators at a theatrical performance.

For a number of reasons the impact of the operatic style on church music in Lutheran Germany was less rapid and less radical in nature. In the first place Opera was essentially an Italian creation and it was some time before the new form became firmly established in other countries. During the greater part of the seventeenth century there was in Germany (despite the isolated example of Schütz's *Dafne* of 1627) no native Opera, and the country relied for its rare operatic productions mainly on works which were imported from Italy and France. Also, while the Italians were temperamentally inclined towards theatricality and display, the Germans as a nation were characterized by a fundamental seriousness of mind and spirit, racial characteristics which had of course been heightened and tempered by the terrible ordeal of the Thirty Years' War during the early part of the century. A further, very important reason was the high degree of organization in Lutheran church music which, with its great tradition of the chorale, acted always as a firm defence against rapid and excessive secularization. The growing interrelation between the Church and the theatre in Lutheran Germany was therefore basically different from its counterpart in Italy. Whereas in Italy Opera was originally a purely secular medium of artistic expression which later had repercussions on Catholic church music, in Germany the growth of an indigenous Opera was, from the first, strongly interconnected with the spiritual life and thought of the people.

When, in fact, the first public Opera house in Germany opened at Hamburg in 1678, the work chosen for performance was a *spiritual* Opera, entitled *Adam und Eva*, by the Lübeck composer Johann Theile who has already been mentioned as the composer of a Passion according to St Matthew. The choice of a sacred subject for this Opera is of great significance; whereas the early Italian Opera composers, who were inspired

94

by the ideals of a pre-Christian era, returned for their libretto material to the myths of classical antiquity, the composers of the Protestant north of Germany turned with equal naturalness to stories of the Bible. The reaction in Hamburg to this sacred type of Opera was, on the whole, favourable. Some of the more progressive clergy of the time welcomed the new artform as an important means of spiritual refreshment; for instance Heinrich Elmenhorst, a pastor of Hamburg, in a pamphlet in support of Opera, argued that the form was 'simply the ancient Greek drama applied to Christian ends'. Others were less certain and we find that Anton Reiser, a pastor of St Jacob's, Hamburg, in a publication of 1682, numbered Opera 'amongst the works of the devil'.

By the beginning of the eighteenth century the influence of the operatic style began to show more clearly in Lutheran church music. As a reaction against the subjective simplicity advocated by the Pietists, a Hamburg pastor, Erdmann Neumeister (Reiser's successor at St Jacob's), produced a cycle of cantata texts which were fashioned exactly in the style of Opera libretti. In each cantata in this cycle there were four recitative sections and four arias, all consisting of freely-composed verse; and thus the texts allowed no scope for the use of the more traditional resources of church music. This first cycle was however followed, shortly afterwards, by two further ones which were less extreme in design and presented opportunities for the use of choruses and chorales and even included short passages from the Scriptures. These cantata texts were eagerly welcomed by the leading musicians of Hamburg such as Keiser, Telemann and Mattheson, and were set to music in a brilliant operatic style. Johann Mattheson (1681-1764), an influential critic, author and composer, was a staunch advocate of the theatrical style in church music, claiming that it would 'arouse virtuous passions' by the intensity of its expression. In 1712, in the face of considerable opposition, he introduced women singers into the choir at Hamburg Cathedral; such a step was of course made necessary by the complications of the new musical style which frequently demanded from the singers a prima donna's power and flexibility of voice. Writing later, Mattheson said '. . . at first I was implored not to bring any women into the choir; in the end they could not have enough of them'. Hamburg had rapidly succumbed to the fascinations of the new style.

Before long, Passion composition also began to show the influence of these profound stylistic changes. Not even this most sacred story was safe from the attentions of operatic poets and composers. In an age which was little distinguished for its delicacy of taste, slight heed was paid to the impropriety of presenting the Passion in a wholly theatrical manner. And so the 'Opera' Passion[1] flourished in the theatre at Hamburg as a pious form of entertainment during Lent. Taking their lead from the cantata texts of Neumeister, a number of poets produced Passion libretti in which the Gospel narrative was entirely abandoned in favour of rhymed couplets of a sentimental and artificial nature. Curiously enough, these libretti which, like their models by Neumeister, were part of a reaction against the Pietist cult of simplicity, displayed in many details of language—their tasteless imagery and their preoccupation with the grosser physical aspects of pain and suffering—traits which were characteristic of Pietist poetry. This was, however, an age of great German musicians—not poets; and in many cases the music which was set to these libretti was of fine quality. Reinhard Keiser, a leading Hamburg Opera composer, was, in 1704, the first to compose one of these 'Opera' Passions. The libretto, entitled *Der blutige und sterbende Jesus* (The bleeding and dying Jesus), was the work of C. F. Hunold-Menantes, a disciple of Neumeister. In addition to the normal characters in the Passion story the poet introduced a symbolic figure called the 'Daughter of Zion', whose function was to present lyrical commentary during the unfolding of the story; this character was also adopted by Picander for use in Bach's St Matthew Passion and serves a similar reflective purpose in that work, notably in the alto aria with chorus 'Ah! now is my Saviour gone' which begins the second half. Despite a few shocked protests from members of the Hamburg clergy, this work by Keiser appears to have scored a considerable success and was followed in 1711 by another similar setting *Tränen unter dem Kreuze Jesu* (Weeping under the Cross of Jesus), based on a libretto by J. U. König. By degrees a number of these Passion texts appeared. Outstanding amongst them was

---

[1] The term 'Opera' Passion is used to indicate that these works were based entirely on operatic libretti, as opposed to the Oratorio Passions which were based mainly on the Gospel narratives. These Passions were not actually acted on the stage like true Operas though, in some cases, stage directions were inserted in the libretti to help the audience to visualize the scenes.

a libretto by Barthold Heinrich Brockes, a member of the Hamburg town council, which avoided some of the more blatant literary excesses of its predecessors and provided composers with a well-balanced and varied scheme of construction. In this libretto, *Der für die Sünden der Welt gemarterte und sterbende Jesus* (Jesus martyred and dying for the sins of the world), a concession is made to tradition by the inclusion of chorale verses, though the original narrative of the Gospel account is again rejected in favour of a free poetic version. Musical settings of this text were produced by all the greatest musicians of the day, notably Keiser, Handel, Telemann[1] and Mattheson; at a later date Bach adapted some of the verses of Brockes for inclusion as lyrical interpolations in the St John Passion. In 1715 Keiser produced a fine setting of another Passion libretto by J. U. König, entitled *Der zum Tode verurtheilte und gekreuzigte Jesus* (Jesus condemned to death and crucified), a work which shows the composer at the height of his powers. The music of this setting is characterized by a nobility of style which is in marked contrast to the maudlin sentimentality of much of the text. The following example, with its expressive use of dissonance and pathetic falling semitones, gives a good idea of the sensitivity of Keiser's writing; in style the music shows a clear relationship to the work of his great contemporaries, Handel and Bach, though it is distinguished by many individual traits. (See Example 15 on following page.)

The 'Opera' Passions of Hamburg were however an ephemeral fashion, a rapidly passing phase. Their main weakness lay in their complete rejection of the Gospel text; the lyrical effusions of pious Hamburg poets could in no way compensate for the sacrifice of the majestic language of the Bible. In his Passions Bach reaffirms the importance of the Biblical narrative and so reveals himself as a spiritual heir to the Oratorio Passion tradition of the seventeenth century.

The most important works which bridge the gap between the seventeenth-century Oratorio Passions and those of Bach are the two settings by Handel. In the earlier of these settings, the St John Passion (1704) which was based on a libretto by Postel, important features of the Oratorio type, such as the Evangelist and the literal Gospel text, are retained. The work is very rich in lyrical movements, in the form of arias and

[1] See Appendix X, p. 159, for a fuller discussion of Telemann's Passion music.

Example 15 *Der zum Tode verurtheilte und gekreuzigte Jesus*
R. Keiser

duets, though no use is made of congregational chorales. Particularly fine is the bass aria *O grosses Werk* (O work sublime) which occurs immediately before the death of Jesus. This movement by Handel clearly served as a model for the alto aria 'All is fulfilled' which Bach interpolates at this point in his St John Passion; both these arias end with Jesus's utterance from the Cross 'It is finished' set, with wonderful effect, to the same musical phrase as in the preceding recitative section. Again, the final chorus of this Passion, which is designed as an idealized lullaby to accompany the entombment of the body of Christ, anticipates in a remarkable way the great final choruses in the Bach Passions. Handel's later Passion, which dates from 1716, is a setting of the Brockes Passion libretto mentioned above. In this work there is an even more striking anticipation of the methods of Bach. In the soprano aria 'Haste, ye souls', the solo vocal line is punctuated by choral interjections 'Come where, come where?', a device which is exactly imitated by Bach on three occasions in the great Passions; in the bass aria 'Haste poor souls' (an adaptation of the same words from Brockes's text) from the St John Passion; and in the opening chorus, and the alto aria 'See the Saviour's outstretched Hands' from the St Matthew Passion. In each of these movements the actual words 'Come where?' ('Look where?' in the case of the opening chorus of the St Matthew Passion) are used; a further parallel instance is provided by the duet for soprano and alto 'Behold, my Saviour now is taken' from the St Matthew Passion where, in an exactly similar way, the chorus interject cries of 'Loose Him! leave Him! bind Him not!' (see p. 71.) Bach's knowledge of this work by Handel is proved by the existence of a manuscript copy which is partly in his handwriting.

When we turn to the lyrical arias in the Bach Passions we find, in every case, long and elaborate movements with highly-decorated vocal lines and richly expressive instrumental accompaniments. The arias in the St Matthew Passion are, without being in any way inferior, conceived generally in a simpler and less sophisticated style than those in the St John Passion. Several of these movements in the later work are cast in the Italian operatic *da capo* aria form, which provides for an exact repetition of the opening of the song after a contrasted middle section, thus forming a lucid ternary structure. But in the St John Passion less use is made of this *da capo* form, and the arias show on the whole a greater subtlety and ingenuity of construction. In both Passions there are many striking examples of independent musical phrases in the orchestral accompaniment which are combined contrapuntally with the voice-part and which are used to illustrate figuratively some important word-image in the text. These are found particularly in the arioso recitative movements which precede many of the arias in the St Matthew Passion. In the tenor recitative 'O grief! that bows the Saviour's troubled heart!', the scene is painted by two groups of instruments, 'Grief!' being expressed by a drooping figure played on two flutes and two oboi da caccia, and the 'throbbing' of the Saviour's heart by the repeated semiquavers of the bass strings, organ and *continuo*. In the alto recitative 'O gracious God! Behold, the Saviour standeth bound' which follows the scene of the scourging of Christ, the accompaniment of strings and *cont-*

inuo conjures up a vivid picture of the chastisement by means of a sharp dotted rhythm ♪ ♩♩ ♩ ♪ ♩♩ ♩ which recalls the accompaniment to the words 'He gave His back to the smiters' from the aria 'He was despised' in Handel's *Messiah;* the narrator's vivid *melisma* on the word 'scourged' in the St John Passion, which we have noticed earlier (see p. 50), is in fact also supported by this rhythmic figure in the bass. This figurative use of musical phrases in relation to the text, which was an integral part of Bach's musical language, stems directly from the normal practice of sixteenth-century composers. In the *Plain and Easy Introduction to Practical Music* (1597), Thomas Morley, the famous Elizabethan madrigal composer, writes, 'Moreover you must have a care that when your matter signifieth "ascending", "high", "heaven", and such like, you must make your music ascend; and by the contrary, where your ditty speaketh of "descending", "lowness", "depth", "hell", and others such like, you must make your music descend'.[1] When Bach, in the arioso recitative from the St Matthew Passion 'The Saviour, low before His Father bending', provides an accompaniment of falling semiquavers, he is obeying an instinct as natural as that of any sixteenth-century composer who sets a falling vocal line to the words *Descendit de coelis.*

In the majority of the arias Bach uses the ornamental style of vocal writing which was characteristic of his period. Frequently elaborate vocal *melismas* are used for expressive pictorial purposes to underline the significance of particular words and this of course raises difficult problems when the texts of the Passions are translated into other languages. An appropriate translation of a German phrase may easily result in the stressing of some quite insignificant word by a complicated vocal *roulade.* For example, in the bass aria 'Come, healing Cross' from the St Matthew Passion, there is a phrase '*Wird mir mein Leiden*' in which the significant word '*Leiden*' (suffering) is painted by an elaborate *melisma.* One older English version[2] of the Passion translates this as 'Should burdens e'er . . .' so that the emphasis of the melodic ornamentation falls on the quite unimportant word 'e'er'. In another,

[1] Thomas Morley, *A Plain and Easy Introduction to Practical Music* (edited by R. A. Harman), Dent, 1952, p. 291.
[2] The Stanford edition of 1910, published by Stainer & Bell.

more modern edition,[1] the phrase is neatly reversed and reads
'And if the burdens . . .', so that the word underlined by the
vocal decoration now becomes 'burdens', which corresponds
more closely with the original German. Not all the problems
of translation are as easily solved as this and, though the best
modern editions show remarkable skill in surmounting the
difficulty, the reader is warned against attaching overmuch
significance to apparent examples of word-painting in translated versions of the Passions.

The great meditative choruses which are used by Bach
to frame the Gospel narrative are of course the natural
descendants of the traditional *Introitus* and *Conclusio* in
ancient Passion music. From very early times it had been customary to begin the Passion with an announcement of the title
Passio Domini nostri Jesu Christi secundum Matthaeum (or
whichever Evangelist it was), and to end with a simple offer-
ing of praise and thanks, called by Catholic composers a
Gratiarum Actio and by Lutherans a *Danksagungslied*. In the
St John Passion (1643) by Thomas Selle we find the first signs
of a development of this idea in the interpolation of three
large-scale choral and orchestral *Intermedia* between the
three parts of the work. The first of these movements is based
on the Passion prophecy from Isaiah, chapter fifty-three,
'Surely, He hath borne our griefs', which was later set so
magnificently by Handel in *Messiah*; the second is a version of
'My God, My God, why hast Thou forsaken me?' which is
freely adapted from the twenty-second Psalm; and the third,
which ends the whole work, is an elaborate *concertato* setting
of the Passion chorale *O Lamm Gottes unschuldig*. Later in
the seventeenth century few composers are found to rival the
enterprise of Thomas Selle in this respect, though the motet
settings of chorale texts which conclude the Passions of Schütz
are beautifully and elaborately conceived.

Bach's choruses are broadly-planned movements, based with
one exception on freely-composed lyrical texts; this exception
occurs in the lyrical movement 'Ah! now is my Saviour gone'
which opens the second half of the St Matthew Passion, where
the alto soloist (the Daughter of Zion) sings a free poetic text
while the chorus interpolate short sections based on the
beginning of the sixth chapter of the Song of Solomon,
'Whither is thy beloved gone, O thou fairest among women?'.

[1] The Elgar-Atkins edition of 1938, published by Novello.

The remarkably apt placing of these great Passion choruses was the result of much alteration and experiment by the composer. In its original form the St John Passion began with the chorale fantasia 'O man, thy grievous sin bemoan' which now stands at the end of the first part of the St Matthew Passion. At a later date Bach substituted the fine chorus 'Lord and Master, in all lands the gath'ring nations hail Thee' which, unlike the chorus of lamentation which begins the St Matthew Passion, is a triumphant affirmation of the victory of the Passion. Similarly at the end of the St John Passion, the chorus which originally preceded the final congregational hymn was a movement based on the chorale *Christe, du Lamm Gottes*; this was also removed by the composer and transferred to the end of the church cantata *Du wahrer Gott und Davids Sohn* (1724). The wonderful choruses which now stand at the end of the two Passions are strikingly similar in style; they share the same key (C minor), the same time signature and the same musical form—that of the *da capo* aria.[1] In both these choruses the composer creates an atmosphere of tender resignation by portraying, in a simple and moving manner, the farewells of devout Christians to their dead Saviour, as His body is laid to rest in the tomb.

[1] For the final chorus of the St Matthew Passion Bach adopts the solemn rhythm of the *sarabande*, basing his movement on a theme from an earlier keyboard work which was probably composed at Cöthen.

VIII

THE ROLE OF THE ORCHESTRA

T H E tradition of simplicity and austerity during Holy Week which finds expression in the veiling of church paintings, statues and other artistic adornments, exercised a continual restraint on the development of Passion music. We have already noticed, for example, the apparent reluctance with which the medieval Plainsong Passion eventually yielded place to a more elaborate polyphonic type of setting during the latter part of the fifteenth century. In their turn musical instruments which had frivolous, secular associations, were not readily admitted to the sombre rites of Passiontide.

In other branches of church composition two distinct uses of instruments were common during the Renaissance and early Baroque periods. During the sixteenth century it was quite normal for the voice-parts in a Mass or motet to be supported by instruments which doubled the vocal lines, or even for instruments to be substituted for vocal parts which were missing. The cherished *a cappella* tradition, in which it is assumed that all the vocal polyphonic music of this period was performed with the utmost purity of style by unaccompanied voices, is largely a myth; this misconception arose from the somewhat nostalgic attitude of such men as Johann Fux (1660-1741) the famous theorist, who regarded this music as the product of a lost age of innocence. Nevertheless, because of the solemnity of the sacred rites during Holy Week, it seems unlikely that this *colla parte* (with the voice-part) use of instruments was normally extended to the motet settings of the Passion.

The second use of instruments which developed gradually at the close of the sixteenth century occurred in a mode of composition known as the *stile concertato*; in this style the instruments could be used either together with the voices or separately as an orchestral chorus which would contrast antiphonally with the vocal choirs. Giovanni Gabrieli, who died in 1612, was a pioneer of this style of composition and his brilliant, colourful motets for multiple choirs each with its group of accompanying instruments became an outstanding feature of the services at St Mark's, Venice. One contemporary report refers in particular to the 'grand harmony' which resulted from the use of this opulent musical style in Venice.[1] The influence of this new and vividly expressive type of composition spread rapidly to other European countries where it was cultivated for some time alongside the traditional church style (the *stile antico*) before eventually superseding it. In Germany the new style was eagerly adopted by a host of church composers, notably H. L. Hassler (1564-1612), M. Praetorius (1571-1621), J. H. Schein (1586-1630) and Heinrich Schütz (1585-1672). In 1618, in the first part of his *Opella Nova*, Johann Schein, who succeeded Calvisius as Cantor at St Thomas's Leipzig and was thus one of Bach's most notable predecessors in that office, was amongst the first to show the possibilities of the new *concertato* style when combined with the ancient Lutheran chorale melodies; while in the following year Schütz, who had studied for some years with Gabrieli in Venice, produced a remarkable work entitled *Psalmen Davids* which was composed in the grand Venetian manner for several choirs with instrumental accompaniment.

The earliest surviving example of an instrumentally-accompanied Passion is Thomas Selle's setting of St John which dates from 1643. In view of the severity of the strictures against the use of instruments in Holy Week, it is surprising to find that Selle in this work imitates all the most sumptuous features of Gabrieli's Venetian motets. There is nothing tentative or apologetic about this initial breach of the Passiontide conventions. In the *Introitus* a six-part chorus (with divided altos and tenors) is set antiphonally against a similarly-divided group of soloists, called the *favoriti*, an arrangement which is also maintained in the choral *Intermedia* which separate the three sections of the narrative, though here the chorus is reduced to five real parts (the tenors being combined), and the solo group to three (soprano, tenor and bass). Corresponding to the two choral groups there are two instrumental groups, one employing three violins, two bassoons and organ *continuo*,

[1] A. Pirro, *H. Schütz* (*Les Maîtres de la Musique*), Paris, 1913 (1924), p. 19.

and the other, two cornetti (an obsolete type of woodwind instrument with a cup mouthpiece similar to a trumpet), a flute, two viole da gamba, and a regal (a portable type of organ similar in appearance to a harmonium but possessing a nobler quality of tone). In addition to their combined function as a choral group the soloists also each portray one of the characters in the drama : the soprano represents the maid, the two altos Pilate and the servant, the two tenors the Evangelist and Peter, and the bass Jesus. For his accompaniment of these solo characters Selle uses an elaborate scheme of instrumental characterization. The Evangelist is accompanied by two bassoons (or, alternatively, two archilutes), Jesus by two violins, Peter and the servant by two flutes and bassoon (or trombone), and Pilate, with a splendidly aristocratic effect, by two cornetti and trombone.[1] This work has no parallel amongst the Passion compositions of this period, either in its use of instruments or in its general musical style; as it lacks the intensely subjective element typical of the majority of Lutheran church compositions, its effect is more that of a splendid musical pageant—imaginative, bold and picturesque, but unfortunately marred at times by an extraordinary ineptitude in the manipulation of the musical details. The only characteristic link with the Lutheran musical tradition lies in the use of the chorale *O Lamm Gottes unschuldig* in the final *Intermedium*. Selle undoubtedly realized that his daring scheme of composition would not be generally acceptable in a work intended for Passiontide performance and he indicated in a lengthy foreword his willingness for the setting to be presented without its more revolutionary features—the *Intermedia* and the instrumental accompaniment. He also gave a number of alternatives for the instruments specified in the score, such as archilutes in place of the bassoons and regal for the accompaniment of the Evangelist.

At this period an orchestra was by no means the highly-organized medium of musical expression that we know to-day. A miscellaneous body of instrumentalists would be assembled for some festive court occasion such as a royal wedding, and after the performance, their services no longer required, they

---

[1] A similar system of instrumental characterization occurs in Schütz's *Christmas History* (1664), in which Herod is accompanied by two trumpets (*clarini*), the chief priests by two trombones and the angel by two violas (*violette*).

would be dismissed. An assembly of so ephemeral a nature necessarily lacked the basic degree of constitution and organization which is an essential feature of an orchestra in the more modern sense. A well-known example of such an 'orchestra' was the one provided by Monteverdi for his Opera *Orfeo*, which was written at the request of the Duke of Mantua and received its first performance at the *Accademia degli Invaghiti* in Mantua in 1607. Operatic performances at that time were exceedingly costly and were forced to depend for patronage almost entirely upon royal or extremely wealthy aristocratic circles; a typical example is Schütz's *Dafne* which was performed in 1627 at the command of the Elector of Saxony who desired a special celebration to mark the occasion of his daughter's marriage. In the case of Monteverdi's *Orfeo* expense was apparently not spared on the orchestra for which the composer demanded at least thirty-seven instruments, including viole da brazzo, tromboni, cornetti and several keyboard instruments such as clavicembali (harpsichords), organi de legno (wooden organs),[1] and a regal. But despite the large number of instruments employed the instrumentation in *Orfeo* is not daringly experimental and Monteverdi, in keeping with contemporary custom, gives specific details of the orchestration only at the more important dramatic moments. There was no parallel at this time to the modern idea of orchestration as an essential part of the composer's function; the normal practice was for the composer to leave the details of the instrumentation to the musician in charge of the performance who would of course have to modify his demands according to the number and quality of the players available. By comparison with many of the orchestral 'scores' of this period Thomas Selle's instrumentation in his St John Passion is remarkably precise and detailed.

The current vagueness in the specification of instruments can be seen in another Passion composition of this period—the *Sieben Worte Christi* (The Seven Last Words from the Cross) by Schütz. In this work the five different instruments required are simply marked *vox suprema, altus, tenor 1, tenor 2,* and *bassus,* though in this case it is fairly clear from the musical context that stringed instruments were intended. The main function of this orchestra is to perform an instru-

[1] These were chamber organs with wooden flue pipes as opposed to the metal reed pipes of the regal.

mental *symphonia* which is placed between the *Introitus* and the beginning of the narrative and again, repeated exactly, between the end of the narrative and the final chorus. This *symphonia* is composed in a smooth, quasi-vocal style, the instrumental parts moving together in massed five-part harmony; but despite its simplicity of style this short movement reveals in its two contexts in the work a stark beauty which is extraordinarily moving. Elsewhere throughout the work the accompaniment is for *continuo* only, except for the words of Christ where the *vox suprema* and *altus* instruments (probably a violin and a viola) add expressive colouring to His speech.

Attention has frequently been called to Bach's beautiful use of the strings of the orchestra as an accompaniment to the words of Jesus in the St Matthew Passion, a device whereby His utterances are singled out from those of all the other characters, who are accompanied by *continuo* only. It cannot however be claimed that Bach was original in the use of this device, as every composer of an instrumentally-accompanied Passion during the seventeenth century similarly selects the Saviour's words for special treatment. Where in fact Bach does depart strikingly from convention is in the St John Passion in which the words of Jesus receive *no* special treatment and are accompanied, like those of the narrator and the minor characters, only by the *continuo*. In the Passions by Sebastiani (1672) and Theile (1673) strings are used as an accompaniment to the narration and to nearly all the utterances of the *dramatis personae*; in these works the part of Jesus is distinguished from the others only by the nature of the stringed instruments which provide the accompaniment, the Saviour's words being accompanied by the sweet-toned violins and those of the other characters by the more reedy-toned viols.

During the seventeenth century the hard fight for supremacy between the ancient viol family and its younger rivals, the violin family, was being gradually decided in favour of the latter instruments. The violin family which first appeared in the early sixteenth century consisted of three main instruments—the violin, the viola, and the violoncello—and originally they were considered frivolous and suitable only for the performance of the lightest types of music; but during the course of the seventeenth century the famous schools of Italian violin makers—G. P. Maggini at Brescia, and Nicolò

Amati, Antonio Stradivari and Giuseppe Guarneri at Cremona —brought these instruments to perfection and ensured their future dominance over all other types of bowed instruments. Apart from their marked difference of tone, mentioned above, the instruments of the viol family differ from those of the violin family in three main respects: (i) they normally have six strings, (ii) they have finger-boards which are fretted to make each note sound like an open string by eliminating the possibility of the fleshy, stopped-string vibrato, and (iii) they are held downward so as to rest on the knee of the performer with a consequent difference in the technique of bowing. As with the violin family, there were three main sizes of instruments—the treble (or discant), the tenor and the bass. In seventeenth-century scores the two families of instruments were frequently distinguished by the terms *da braccio* (of the arm) for the violin, and *da gamba* (of the leg) for the viol, the reference being of course to the position of the instrument in performance. Strictly speaking the term viola *da gamba* should refer to any member of the viol family, but confusion is apt to arise from the fact that the bass instrument, which is similar in pitch to the modern 'cello, outlived its fellows in popularity and appeared in orchestral scores as a solo instrument until late in the eighteenth century. A notable example of such a solo occurs in Bach's St Matthew Passion in the accompaniment to the bass aria *Komm süsses Kreuz* (Come, healing Cross); in this movement the closely-spaced chords and the wide leaps alternating with rapid conjunct figuration are unsuitable for performance on any modern substitute instrument.

By the second half of the seventeenth century stringed instruments (frequently a mixture of violins and viols) became firmly established as the basis of the orchestra. The principal wind instruments in use were the recorders, flutes, oboes, bassoons, trumpets and trombones and their function was to strengthen and add colour to the basic string texture and, more important still, to perform elaborate *obbligato* solos with the support of the strings and *continuo*. It was the custom at this time to associate the various tone-colours of the wind instruments with particular shades of emotional expression and meaning. Recorders for example were frequently associated with pastoral music, while the oboes had funereal, the trombones supernatural and the cornetts aristocratic connotations.

The trumpets were associated with brilliance and festivity and so of course were never used in Passion music. As a rule, when an *obbligato* instrument was used to accompany the voice in an aria, the choice would fall on the one which most nearly corresponded in tone-colour with the main emotional idea which characterized the whole song. Many examples of this system of emotional colouring by instrumentation are to be found in the church compositions of Bach.

In the St Matthew Passion (*c.* 1700) by Johann Meder which is scored for two recorders, two oboes, two violins and *continuo*, the general accompaniment of the choir is provided by the oboes, strings and *continuo*, while the recorders are reserved for occasional solo appearances; a notable instance occurs in the first part of the work where a solo recorder, true to its pastoral nature, features in a solemn *symphonia* during the scene in the Garden at Gethsemane. There is actually no occasion in this work where the recorders and the oboes both play together, a fact which suggests that the same musicians were probably expected to perform on both instruments. It is quite certain that, in Bach's time also, orchestral players were frequently required to perform on several instruments of diverse techniques, and that this was often detrimental to their real mastery of any single instrument. In a memorandum addressed to the Leipzig town council, dated August 23rd, 1730, Bach complains about the difficulty of obtaining suitable instrumentalists for the maintenance of a 'well-appointed church music'; as is not surprising, one of the chief obstacles is the inadequacy of the salaries offered. Bach contrasts the position at Leipzig with the more favourable conditions which exist at Dresden, where the musicians are 'paid by His Royal Majesty' and are thus 'relieved of all concern for their living, free from chagrin, and obliged each to master *but a single instrument*'. (my italics). With instruments demanding the same technique of performance the case was of course different; an oboe-player for example would naturally be expected to be equally proficient on the two alto versions of his instrument—the oboe d'amore and the oboe da caccia— just as the modern oboe player is frequently required to be an equally capable performer on the cor anglais. Bach's actual resources at this time seem to have been slender indeed : three violins, two oboes, two trumpets, and a bassoon—played by the 'apprentice'! Nor indeed was the skill of the players above suspicion. 'Modesty,' writes Bach, 'forbids me to speak at all truthfully of their qualities and musical knowledge. Nevertheless it must be remembered that they are partly *emeriti* and partly not at all in such *exercitio* as they should be'. As this memorandum was written only one year after the first performance of the St Matthew Passion with its elaborate instrumental requirements, it is clear that the Leipzig churches must have suffered a sudden decline in their musical resources.

In Bach's St John Passion the basic accompanying orchestra consists of two flutes, two oboes, bassoons (which double the violoncellos), strings and organ *continuo*. This orchestra doubles the voices in the congregational chorales and in many of the crowd choruses; as a rule all the wind instruments are used to strengthen the melody in the chorale settings, while the four string parts double the soprano, alto, tenor and bass voices at the appropriate pitch. For the accompaniment to the solo arias there is a rich and varied use of *obbligato* instruments, normally combined in pairs. A strikingly beautiful example of scoring occurs in the bass arioso 'Come, ponder, O my soul' (after the scene of the scourging of Christ) in which the voice is supported by two viole d'amore, lute and *continuo*. The lute, which for over two centuries before Bach had held a pre-eminent place amongst accompanying instruments, was by the early eighteenth century rapidly losing favour. Bach's choice of the instrument for this movement is a clear indication of his sensitivity to the subtleties of instrumental colouring, though he acknowledges the obsolete nature of the instrument by providing an alternative version of its part for the harpsichord.[1] The viola d'amore, a pair of which are also used in the succeeding aria 'Behold Him : See! His back all torn and bleeding', is another comparative rarity in Bach's scores. The instrument's chief characteristic, its sweet and silvery tone, arises from the use of wire strings placed beneath the fingerboard which vibrate in sympathy with the normal gut strings placed above. At the end of the Passion, the pathos of the arioso 'My heart, behold the world intent' and the aria 'O heart, melt in weeping' which follow the rending of the veil of the temple, is underlined by the use

---

[1] At a later date, after 1730, Bach produced a further version of this part for organ; the part was marked 'To be played on the organ with eight and four foot Gedackt'.

of oboi da caccia—literally oboes 'of the hunt'. This instrument, which is an alto version of the oboe and thus akin to the modern cor anglais, is notable for its peculiarly sombre and mournful tone-colour. Comparatively little *obbligato* use is made of stringed instruments in the St John Passion; the most notable example occurs in the alto aria 'All is fulfilled' in which there is a long and elaborately ornamented solo for a viola da gamba.

In the St Matthew Passion, Bach uses two accompanying orchestras—one for each of the two choirs—an arrangement which recalls that of Thomas Selle in his St John Passion, though the elaborate polyphonic technique employed by Bach is in sharp contrast to the massive chordal structures of the earlier composer. The basic instrumental requirements for *each* of these orchestras are two flutes, two oboes, strings, and organ and harpsichord *continuo*. In the memorandum to the Leipzig town council of 1730, mentioned above, Bach states as his minimum requirements for the strings of the orchestra 'two or even three' first and second violins, four violas, two violoncelli, and one violone (equivalent to the modern double-bass); thus, including the wind instruments and the two organs, at least sixteen performers would be required for each orchestra. Two organs seems an impossibly extravagant demand; but it is in fact known that there were two organs in St Thomas's Church during Bach's tenure of office as Cantor. One of the instruments appears to have been in a very poor state of repair and of very little use, but according to the records of J. C. Rost, who was custodian of St Thomas's at this time, both the organs were used for the Passion performance in 1736. It seems likely however that at the first performance of the St Matthew Passion in 1729 one organ had to do duty for both the orchestras.

As in the St John Passion, a wide range of emotional colouring is imparted to the numerous reflective movements by the use of *obbligato* instruments. The soprano recitative and aria which follow the scene of the Institution of the Holy Communion are accompanied most expressively by two oboi d'amore which portray the mood indicated by the words 'Although our eyes o'erflow, since Jesus now must from us go' from the recitative movement. The oboe d'amore, unlike the normal oboe and the oboe da caccia, was not a true descendant of the ancient shawm family and first came into use early in the eighteenth century. Slightly deeper in pitch than an oboe, it is sweeter in tone than the oboe da caccia but possesses less deeply pathetic and poignant powers of expression. Oboi da caccia do in fact appear in many of the most deeply sorrowful movements in the Passion, such as the tenor arioso 'O grief! that bows the Saviour's troubled heart' during the scene at Gethsemane, and the soprano recitative and aria 'For love my Saviour now is dying' which occurs after Pilate's question 'Why, what evil hath he done?'. In the latter aria the chief solo instrument is actually the flute and the two oboi da caccia provide a simple background of repeated chords; this is the only movement in the entire work in which the *continuo* is silent throughout—the three wood-wind instruments suffice here to supply a complete harmonic accompaniment for the voice. In addition to the viola da gamba solo which accompanies the bass solo 'Come, healing Cross', mentioned above, there are several examples of *obbligato* solos for stringed instruments; outstanding amongst these is the wonderfully expressive violin solo which appears in the alto aria 'Have mercy, Lord, on me' after the scene of Peter's denial. In this movement the vocal and instrumental parts are so inextricably interwoven that it is impossible not to regard them as two equal and balanced voices in a perfectly blended duet. Frequently a melodic phrase, announced by the solo alto, is immediately answered and continued or decorated contrapuntally by the wordless voice of the solo violin; in its rich harmonies and intricate decorative patterns this aria represents one of the highest flights of Bach's creative imagination.

We have noticed earlier several instances of the symbolical use of instrumental colouring to underline the moods and emotions expressed in lyrical arias; but there are also two particular points of climax in the Passion story in which the orchestra can embellish the drama by direct and vivid realistic representation—the crowing of the cock during the scene of Peter's denial, and the rending of the Temple veil and the earthquake after the scene of the death of Jesus. During the early part of the eighteenth century many composers began to show a developing awareness of the possibilities inherent in instrumental music for realistic mimicry. Johann Kuhnau, Bach's immediate predecessor at St Thomas's, Leipzig, achieved considerable fame with his Biblical sonatas for harpsichord—

David and Goliath, The Marriage of Jacob, The Healing of Hezekiah and so on—in which he attempted to give realistic imitations of dramatic events, such as the flight of the stone from David's sling, and the downfall of Goliath. In the normal way Bach shows little interest in this rather naïve type of realism; but in the case of these two scenes in the Passion settings, the composer weaves a popular realistic element beautifully and unobtrusively into the texture. In the St John Passion, the crowing of the cock is discreetly marked by a rapid arpeggio figure played on the accompanying *continuo* instrument; while, in the later Passion, a similar upward arpeggio figure is actually sung by the Evangelist with a remarkably vivid and life-like effect. Spitta[1] has drawn attention to the popular Passion-play tradition in Germany in which the crowing of the cock was often realistically reproduced by an oboe or similar wind instrument, and was a much appreciated point of climax; he suggests, with considerable likelihood, that Bach may have been influenced, either consciously or unconsciously, by this living tradition of the people. Undoubtedly the more austere traditions of the church liturgy permitted some degree of realism at this point, as many of the earlier Passions, notably those of Schütz, Sebastiani, Theile and Meder, contain more or less life-like *melismas* which are sung by the Evangelist to represent the crowing of the cock. (See Appendix VII, p. 147)

In the case of the earthquake scene a really vivid representation can only be achieved by the use of an orchestra. In the older unaccompanied type of Passion, the usual practice was for the Evangelist simply to describe the scene without any attempt at pictorial realism. Bach's settings of this scene in the two Passions are remarkably similar; the setting in the St Matthew Passion is the more elaborate of the two and might well be regarded as a polished and perfected version of that in the earlier work. Two distinct musical ideas are involved; rapidly rushing scales to portray the rending of the Temple veil and a deep shuddering *tremolando* on the lower strings to represent the quaking of the earth.[2] In the St John

[1] P. Spitta, *J. S. Bach* (Translated by Clara Bell and J. A. Fuller-Maitland), Novello, 1951, Vol. 2, pp. 556-7. (pub. in U.S.A. by Dover)

[2] An interesting early use of the string *tremolando* is alleged to have occurred in the lost St Matthew Passion (1664) by Thomas Strutius; in this case the effect was used to heighten the drama of the death of Judas.

Passion the Evangelist presents the complete account of the rending of the Temple veil against an accompaniment of held chords on the *continuo* instrument and this is followed by a single downward-rushing scale which ends on a *tremolando*; this *tremolando* then forms the basis of the accompaniment for the account of the earthquake. Much greater pictorial vividness is achieved in the St Matthew Passion by the use of four upward and downward-rushing scales which actually interrupt the words of the narrator as he describes the rending of the Temple veil. In two seventeenth-century Oratorio Passions there are notable attempts to produce a realistic setting of this scene which make an interesting comparison with Bach's versions. In the St Matthew Passion (1673) by Johann Theile there is a novel but rather unconvincing attempt to portray the terrors of the earthquake by the use of rapidly-repeated semiquavers on the viols which accompany the words of narration; while in the Passion (*c.* 1700) by Johann Meder the quaking of the earth is most imaginatively mingled with the quaking of the awe-struck spectators as the Evangelist gives stammering utterance to his account of the prodigy:

Example 16   (a) *St Matthew Passion* (1673)   J. Theile
              (b) *St Matthew Passion* (*c.* 1700)   J. Meder

(Trans.: And the earth did quake.)

In Bach's St John Passion the earthquake scene is followed by a tenor arioso based on the following stanza which is freely adapted from Brockes:

> My heart, behold the world intent
> A share in Jesu's pain to borrow:
> The sun in sable shroud of sorrow,
> The severed veil, the mountains rent,

The quaking earth, the dead returning,
Their Maker cold in death are mourning.
Wilt thou, my heart, do now thy part?

The accompaniment to this arioso movement is supplied by
two flutes and two oboi da caccia which sustain long chords,
and by the strings which echo the picturesque effects of the
previous dramatic section. During the first three lines of the
stanza the upper strings quietly maintain an intermittent
tremolando; then at the words 'the severed veil' there is a
repetition of the swift downward scale, and this is followed
by a turbulent arpeggio figure which paints the phrase 'the
mountains rent'. By means of this transference of the
orchestral realism, Bach succeeds in blending his lyrical interpolation imperceptibly with the dramatic Gospel narrative,
and provides a perfect connecting-link with the purely meditative aria 'My heart, melt in weeping' which then follows.
But great though the stroke of genius is here, it is transcended
by an even more sublime inspiration in the St Matthew
Passion. In the later work Bach provides no lyrical interpolation after the earthquake scene but proceeds directly to a
wonderfully solemn and exalted setting of the crowd's words
'Truly this was the Son of God'. Whereas in the St John
Passion our thoughts are focused on the wondrous upheaval
of nature, in the later Passion the composer penetrates right
to the heart of the mystery by directing our attention to the
divinity of its Author.

IX

SOLI DEO GLORIA[1]

BACH was the last of the great church musicians. He holds
a position in the history of the Lutheran Church equivalent
to that of Palestrina in the Catholic Church. Since the death
of these two composers the liturgies of their respective
Churches have been enriched by much fine music, but no
composer of the first rank has devoted all, or even the greater
part, of his creative energies to church composition. There are
many reasons for this, some of which are concerned with the
development of musical technique and some with the changing position of the composer in relation both to the Church
and to society in general.

In Palestrina's time a professional musician had little choice
but to serve the Church; apart from a few royal or aristocratic
courts, no other important social institution valued his services
so highly or could offer him so secure a means of livelihood.
And as a natural result of this widespread musical patronage
by the Church the liturgical forms—notably the Mass and the
motet—were pre-eminent and commanded the highest creative
endeavours of musicians. But from the beginning of the seventeenth century, with the amateur-inspired growth of Opera
and Oratorio and such allied instrumental forms as the con-
certo and the sonata, professional musicians rapidly discovered
new scope for employment in the sphere of cultural entertainment. From this time much of the musical patronage
which had formerly belonged exclusively to the Church was
surrendered to or shared by the wealthy aristocracy or even—
as in the case of the public Opera at Venice—the world of
commerce. And composers, no longer bound by the restraints
of the church liturgy—brevity, formalism and restrictions of

---

[1] 'To God alone be the glory'. It was Bach's regular custom to
inscribe this dedicatory motto at the end of the scores of his sacred
compositions.

116

text and personal expression—eagerly accepted the limitless opportunities for experiment and expansion which were offered by the new secular musical forms.

As we have seen earlier, Lutheran Germany reacted more slowly to these developments than the Catholic countries of southern Europe; so closely was the pattern of the Lutheran faith woven into the life of the country that a radical stylistic revolution was readily averted. The Lutheran liturgy, lacking the weighty, age-old traditions of Catholicism, showed a remarkable liberalism and elasticity in its ready absorption of new artistic ideals without a complete sacrifice of the old. Music had always held a favoured position in the Lutheran Church; almost alone amongst religious reformers Luther had pointed the way towards a rich and artistic form of liturgical worship by his reverence for tradition, which is evident in his unwillingness to reject completely the wonderful musical heritage of the ancient Church, and by his recognition that artistic elaboration is not necessarily incompatible with simplicity and sincerity of faith. The fruits of such liberal doctrines were the rich inheritance of Bach.

While Bach, like Palestrina, was essentially a professional church musician, this in no way interfered with his cultivation of purely secular vocal and instrumental music, composed in the same style as his sacred music and for the same purpose—the honouring of God. In common with numerous German musicians of his time he underwent several arduous stages of professional training before emerging finally as a complete master of his art; and armed with these professional skills he devoted himself naturally to the service of the faith in which he had been reared. Musical life in Germany at this time was highly organized; in most large towns and cities the administration of the music in the great Lutheran churches and schools was undertaken by carefully-selected Cantors. The duties of these ubiquitous Cantors however far exceeded those of mere organization; continually they were called upon to make new creative contributions to the living liturgical art of the country. The majority of the Cantors were workaday composers of considerable but not really outstanding talents; though achieving perhaps little personal recognition, they each made a worthy contribution to the musical life of their time. But Bach was a great, a universal genius; and while working within the same social pattern and sharing the same religious views as his lesser contemporaries, he created a musical interpretation of life which transcends all limitations of time, place and creed. It probably never occurred to him to question the ideals and conventions of his epoch, or to speculate on the probable judgment of his music by posterity. And, indeed, why should it have done? As a professional church musician his duty lay in the regular composition of new works for particular church occasions as they arose. And as a deeply religious man he naturally saw fit to employ every worthy musical technique at his command—complex formal structure, intricate melodic ornamentation, abstruse symbolism—for the praise of his Creator. Thus, for Bach, the composition of Passion music was simply a part of his manifold duties as a church composer, the fulfilment of an immediate liturgical need. And for this purpose he naturally adopted the conventional styles and techniques of his period, heightening and illuminating them with the force of his genius.

In the gradual process of evolution from its earliest origins Passion composition had acquired by Bach's time not only many new features of musical form and expression but also quite different liturgical functions. In its earliest Plainsong, Dramatic and Motet forms, the Passion was an integral part of the celebration of the Mass during Holy Week and was therefore necessarily short and ritualistic in style. Such individual characteristics as were displayed by these musical forms arose from the inherently dramatic nature of the Gospel narratives which could not be disguised even in the abstract motet style. The most perfect examples of this objective, ceremonial form of Passion composition are the Latin Dramatic Passions of Victoria, Lassus and Byrd, the German Motet Passions of Lechner and Demantius and the great settings by Heinrich Schütz. But during the seventeenth century the development, particularly within the Lutheran Church, of the Oratorio type of Passion with its pronounced emphasis on devotional meditation, brought about radical alterations in the strict liturgical functions of the genre. The Oratorio itself was not a liturgical form but rather a species of religious entertainment, a sacred counterpart of Opera; and under its influence Passion music increased greatly in size and developed new powers of dramatic and emotional expression which were quite alien to the abstract, symbolical style of the ancient church ritual. Consequently a new type of Holy Week service was evolved in the Lutheran Church which was concerned entirely with the musical presentation of the Passion story, now regarded as a complete form of worship in its own right. At St Thomas's, Leipzig, in Bach's time, the usual form of this Good Friday service was as follows:

(i) Hymn: *Da Jesus an dem Kreuze stund*
(ii) The Passion—Part I
(iii) Hymn: *O Lamm Gottes unschuldig*
(iv) Pulpit hymn: *Herr Jesu Christ, dich zu uns wend*
(v) The Sermon
(vi) The Passion—Part II
(vii) Motet: *Ecce quomodo moritur justus* (Gallus)
(viii) The Passion collect
(ix) Hymn: *Nun danket alle Gott*
(x) The Blessing.

When we recollect that a setting such as Bach's St Matthew Passion lasts by itself over three and a half hours in performance, we cannot but marvel at the powers of endurance displayed by Lutheran congregations in the early eighteenth century.

The great expansion of the Passion form in Bach's time resulted, as we have seen, mainly from the custom of interpolating in the Gospel account numerous musical settings of non-Biblical poetic texts; and it was this very feature which was chiefly responsible for the rapid decay of the form after Bach. Bach was unique for his time in his recognition of the fact that the realistic drama of the Gospel narrative is an essential distinguishing feature of the Passion form. Much of the greatness of his Passion settings lies in the wonderful fusion of dramatic and meditative elements which exist as distinct entities and are yet blended with perfect artistry. But later composers showed a regrettable tendency to sacrifice the essential dramatic element and set the Passion story in an entirely meditative style. In Bach's time Opera and Oratorio were virtually indistinguishable in musical structure and in their use of highly stylized idioms; and consequently the techniques of the theatre—recitative, aria and dramatic chorus —could be used in Passion composition without any gross violation of the restraints of the church liturgy. But as the eighteenth century progressed Opera composers such as Gluck and Mozart discovered new methods of blending lyrical music with realistic drama and created increasingly vivid and naturalistic modes of expression; while Oratorio composers on the other hand favoured a suppression of the dramatic element in favour of the purely contemplative. As a result of this stylistic separation between the two forms, Passion composers were forced to sacrifice the essential dramatic characteristics of the story which, in a frankly realistic Opera form, would plainly have been tasteless and irreverent, and treat the sacred drama in a purely meditative Oratorio fashion. The most notable example of an attempt to continue the Lutheran Passion tradition in this way was a work by C. H. Graun (1704-1759) entitled *Der Tod Jesu* (The death of Jesus) which, lacking the dramatic narrative of the Gospels, can offer only sentimentality and a banal display of religiosity.

A further reason for the decay of the Passion form lay in the rapid decline during the eighteenth century of the great cultural traditions of Lutheran Germany. After the death of Bach in 1750, the new generations of creative musicians who were to shape the future destiny of music belonged mainly to the Catholic south of Europe—notably the Viennese school of Haydn, Mozart, Beethoven and Schubert. For their church compositions these composers turned naturally to the great texts of the Catholic ritual, such as the Mass and the Requiem, and liturgical Passion music, which in the previous era had acquired such peculiarly Protestant associations, was of course neglected.[1] By the time of Mendelssohn's revival of the St Matthew Passion in 1829, all real creative contact with the older culture had been lost and musicians were astonished at this revelation of the hidden treasures of the past. Since then it has taken many years of patient rediscovery to arrive at even a partial recognition of the scope of Bach's achievement.

Bach is generally regarded as being the end of a musical epoch, as being, to paraphrase Beethoven's celebrated dictum,[2]

---

[1] Haydn's short Oratorio *The Seven Words of the Saviour from the Cross* was originally a set of seven slow movements for orchestra which were composed in 1785 for performance during the Three Hours' Devotion in Cadiz Cathedral. The composer later made two arrangements of the work; one, in 1787, for string quartet, and the other, in 1796, for vocal soloists, chorus and orchestra.

[2] '*Nicht Bach, sondern Meer sollte er heissen . . .*' (He should be called an ocean, not a brook . . .)

the great ocean into which all the streams of earlier musical
endeavour flow. But nothing could be more misleading than
to regard all the composers of the era immediately preceding
Bach's as mere 'forerunners'. The evolution of an art such
as music is not simply a continuous process of development
and improvement. We cannot say for example that Haydn is a
better composer than Byrd, or Wagner than Mozart; the
supremacy of such composers arises, irrespective of their
period in musical history, from the perfect balance and fusion
which they attain between musical form and content, between
ideas and techniques of expression. As we have seen in our
consideration of earlier Passion composition, the wonderfully-
moulded musical language in which Bach expresses his
thoughts was the outcome of the labours of many lesser men;
but if we accept perfection of expression within any given
medium as a criterion of greatness, such a composer as Schütz
must certainly be ranked as a classic master. It may well be
that as we approach more nearly to a true assessment of
Bach's greatness we shall be compelled to pay greater heed to
the value of the achievements of his predecessors.

APPENDICES

I. LETTER-SYMBOLS IN PASSION MUSIC *(see page 22)*

The term *synagoga* is a useful one for identifying a specific group of characters in the Passion story (the crowd, the band of disciples and all the single characters except Christ) and is retained in the body of this book for that purpose. It is, however, important to point out that the term has no foundation in ancient liturgical writings but stems from a more recent misinterpretation. In the earliest form of the Plainsong Passion, in which a single chanter by himself presented the entire Gospel account, letter-symbols were placed beside the various sections of the text to show how the separate character-utterances were to be differentiated in pitch, tempo and style of performance. These are the so-called Romanian letters, the first use of which has been associated with the legendary singer, Romanus, who is supposed to have introduced Gregorian chant at St Gall at about the end of the eighth century. When, from the fifteenth century, it became the normal practice for three persons (a priest, a deacon and a sub-deacon) to present the various rôles in the Passion, these letter-symbols were retained and customarily interpreted as follows: c = *cantor* or *chronista*, s = *synagoga* or *succentor*, and † = *Christus*. But in reality the original, correct interpretation of the symbols is quite different. The letter c stands for *celeriter* (quickly) and the letter s for *sursum* (in a raised voice); while the little cross (†) is not in fact a cross at all but simply the letter t standing for *trahere* (to drag) or *tenere* (to hold), indicating that the music for the part of Christ should be performed slowly and reverently.[1]

[1] See Karl Young, *The Drama of the Medieval Church*, 1933, Vol. I, p. 550; also Gustave Reese, *Music in the Middle Ages*, New York, 1940, p. 140, and the article *Passion* in *Die Musik in Geschichte und Gegenwart*, Basel, 1962, Vol. 10, p. 886 et seq.

In various printed missals for Sarum use other letter-symbols are found, indicating the voice-pitches of the various participants in the drama. These are as follows: a = *alta vox* (all crowd groups and single characters except Christ), m = *media vox* (the narrator) and b = *bassa vox* (Christ). In this case also the symbols were originally designed as a guide to a single chanter so that he might, by changes of pitch, achieve some degree of characterization in his presentation of the Gospel story. The Burntisland edition of the Sarum Missal gives the following rubric (col. 264) which indicates the method of performance:

Sequitur Passio. Et est notandum quod triplice voce debet cantari aut pronuntiari; scilicet voce alta, bassa, et media. Quia omnia quae in Passione continentur aut verba sunt Judaeorum vel discipulorum, aut verba sunt Christi, aut Evangelistae narrantis. Quare scire debes quod ubi a litteram invenies verba esse Judaeorum vel discipulorum, quae alta voce sunt proferenda. Ubi vero b invenies verba sunt Christi, quae bassa voce pronuntianda sunt. Ubi vero m invenies verba sunt Evangelistae, quae mediocri voce legenda aut cantanda sunt. Et haec omnia in aliis Passionibus observa.

(Translation: Here follows the Passion. And it is to be noted that it ought to be sung or recited in a three-fold pitch, namely high, low and intermediate pitch. Because all the things which are contained in the Passion are the words either of the Jews or the disciples, or are the words of Christ, or of the Evangelist narrator. Wherefore you should know that where you find the letter *a*, the words are those of the Jews or disciples and are to be uttered at a high pitch. Where you find *b*, the words are those of Christ and are to be pronounced at a low pitch. Where you find *m*, the words are those of the Evangelist and are to be read or sung at an intermediate pitch. And observe all these things in other Passions.)

II. THE EARLIEST POLYPHONIC PASSIONS (*see page 24*)

The Meaux Abbey Passions

The two anonymous fifteenth-century Passions according to St Matthew and St Luke in the British Museum Egerton manuscript 3307 are three-voice settings of the passages normally allotted in Plainsong Passions to the *alta vox*—the utterances of the disciples, of the Jewish mob and of all the single characters in the drama except Christ. The manuscript of the St Luke Passion is complete whereas that of the St Matthew is imperfect at the end.[1] In addition to the two Passions the manuscript also contains fragments of a Mass, hymns, versicles and antiphons, and a number of settings of English carols. Because of the dialect in the carol texts the manuscript is thought to have originated in Yorkshire, probably at Meaux Abbey; one particular carol refers in fact to the Yorkshire village of Hye (Hyth) which used to belong to this Cistercian House. It seems likely that the manuscript was compiled during the reign of Henry VI and should be dated *c.* 1450 (see M. Bukofzer, *Studies in Medieval and Renaissance Music*, New York, 1950, p. 114 et seq.).

The three-voice polyphonic passages in the Passions are technically quite simple, being set in triple time throughout and mainly in a note-against-note declamatory style, showing in places a primitive type of *fauxbourdon* writing with successive six-three chords. The basic mode underlying both settings is mixolydian, the short passages normally cadencing on the final G or on the dominant D. Nevertheless there are some places where final or intermediate cadences fall on other degrees of the mode, such as A, E, or F sharp. These less precisely defined cadences seem to be used with a fairly clear interpretative purpose, usually indicating (as in the comparable case of the cadence formulae in plainchant—see p. 47) the presence of a question mark or of an emphatic exclamation such as Peter's '*O homo non sum*' (Man, I am not); see Example 17.

At the same time there is little evidence of harmony, rhythm or texture being directed to specifically dramatic ends, and such vivid crowd utterances as '*Crucifige eum*' (Crucify him) are set in a simple, ritualistic manner. The identity of style between the two works, noticeable in details of the harmony and in the consistent use of triple-time patterns, suggests strongly that one composer was responsible for both settings. Two very similar Passions (according to St Matthew and St

---

[1] A transcription of all the polyphonic sections in the St Luke Passion is given in M. Bukofzer, *A Newly-Discovered 15-Century Manuscript of the English Chapel Royal*, Part II, Musical Quarterly, 33 (1947), pp. 43-51.

Example 17 *St Luke Passion (c. 1450)* Anon.:.Meaux Abbey

O — ho—— mo non —

sum.

John), dating from about the same period as those in the Egerton MS., are to be found in MS. VI of Shrewsbury School. In these works, also, there are three-voice polyphonic settings of the *turbae* and of the utterances of all the single characters except Christ.

The Modena Passions

Closely challenging the claim of the Meaux Abbey Passions as the earliest to include sections of polyphony are the two anonymous Italian Passions—according to St Matthew and St John—which are preserved in Modena, Biblioteca Estense, MS. Lat. 455 (M.I.12); in fact they were probably written slightly later and may be dated *c.* 1490. Unlike the English settings these Italian works contain polyphonic versions of only the group utterances (those of the disciples, the Jewish mob, the soldiers, etc.); the sayings of the minor solo characters are supplied in the manuscript with the traditional Gregorian plainchant, while no specific music is written down for the rôles of the Narrator and Christ. The majority of the polyphonic sections are set, like those in the Meaux Abbey works, for three voices, using the characteristic *fauxbourdon* technique and with the Passion tones allocated to the discant part. But special interest attaches to the St Matthew Passion because

126

it contains three sections laid out for considerably larger forces, one section à 8 (the actual texture consisting mainly of paired voices), and two fully scored sections à 6. A striking feature of the manuscript is its size which is sufficiently large to permit a considerable number of people to sing from it at the same time. As Bukofzer has pointed out, the richly scored passages in the St Matthew Passion are amongst 'the earliest fully chorus-conscious compositions for six voices' (See M. Bukofzer, *Studies in Medieval and Renaissance Music*, New York, 1950, p. 185).

Example 18 shows, in modern transcription, the six-voice setting of the disciples' questioning utterance '*Ubi vis paremus tibi comedere Pascha?*' (Where wilt thou that we prepare for thee to eat the Passover?). The appropriate plainchant Passion

Example 18   *St Matthew Passion (c. 1490)*

Anon.: Modena, Bibl. Est.

tone is placed in the tenor line, with the characteristic step-wise motion up to the final to indicate the presence of a question mark.

The St Matthew Passion by Richard Davy

Like the Meaux Abbey Passions, Davy's St Matthew is a setting of all the gospel passages normally allotted to the *alta vox*, the utterances of groups and of all single characters apart from Christ; it has the distinction of being the earliest poly-phonic Passion by a known composer. The work, which appeared originally in the famous Eton Manuscript (compiled *c.* 1500), is available in a modern edition by Frank Ll. Harrison in Musica Britannica, Vol. 12, *The Eton Choirbook III*, p. 112. The setting is for four voices (treble, mean, tenor and bass) and shows a degree of technical skill and dramatic aptness far in advance of the Meaux Abbey works. Unfortunately the manuscript is imperfect, the first eleven choral sections being entirely missing and the succeeding twelve choruses lacking the treble and tenor parts; in the modern edition the opening

choruses have been supplied by the skilful adaptation of surviving music from later on in the work, while the pairs of
missing voices have been filled in editorially. The Passion tones
set for the recitation of the parts of the Evangelist and Christ
are those for the Sarum use (which are, incidentally, printed
complete for the first time in Harrison's modern edition). As
with the Gregorian Passion tones, the reciting-notes are C for
the Evangelist and F for Christ. Endings are marked by the

Example 19   *St Matthew Passion* (c. 1500)   R. Davy

fall of a semitone to B for the Evangelist and by the fall of a
minor third to D for the part of Christ, while questions are
indicated in the part of Christ by a rising semitone from E to F.
The recurrent final note B in the Evangelist's part produces a
curious tritonal relationship when followed by the F reciting-
note for the words of Christ. Jesus's cry from the cross 'Heloy,
heloy, lama zabathani', which customarily receives special
plainsong treatment, is marked in the Sarum version to be
taken by 'a third voice' at the high pitch (top E and F) normally
allotted to the *alta vox*.

Some idea of the dramatic character and richly polyphonic style of Davy's choruses can be gained from Example 19 where the Jewish mob, mocking Jesus, cry 'Thou that destroyest the temple, and buildest it in three days, save thyself. If thou be the Son of God, come down from the cross'. Frank Ll. Harrison has pointed out that the presence of a rood-loft, or *pulpitum*, in many of the larger medieval churches may well have had an interesting effect upon performances of Passions such as Davy's St Matthew. On the principal days of the Church's Year it was the normal practice to chant the Epistle and Gospel from the rood-loft, the singers being placed above the choir door, facing towards, but at some distance from, the altar. During Holy Week the various Passion accounts would also be chanted thus. But when choral settings of the *alta vox* rôle were performed these would be sung from the choir floor, thus producing an intriguing spatial effect in relation to the chanters who would continue to present the parts of the Evangelist and Christ from the rood-loft. An excellent gramophone recording of Davy's Passion has recently been issued (Argo ZRG 558, stereo) which re-creates this effect of spacing.

III. DRAMATIC AND MOTET PASSION *(see page 25)*

In his pioneer work (*Die ältere Passionskomposition*, Gütersloh, 1893) Otto Kade divided the polyphonic Passion settings of the sixteenth century into two basic categories. A broad distinction was made between those works—the so-called Dramatic Passions—in which only the crowd utterances and (more rarely) the sayings of the various individual characters are set polyphonically, and those in which the complete Gospel story, comprising all the words of narration as well as the utterances of the crowd and of all the single characters including Jesus, is set in polyphonic motet style—the so-called Motet Passions. More recent research, however, particularly into Passions of Italian origin, has revealed so much variety of style and structure within these fundamental categories that it has become necessary to coin some new terminology in order to achieve greater clarity of definition. In recent writings German musicologists have increasingly referred to three main types of setting which they call the Responsorial Passion, the Through-composed Passion and the Motet Passion, and have furthermore shown that, within the various groups, there are additional sub-species with distinguishing characteristics of form and texture (see Kurt von Fischer, *Zur Geschichte der Passionskomposition des 16. Jahrhunderts in Italien*, AfMW 11 (1954), pp. 189-205; Arnold Schmitz, *Zur motettischen Passion des 16. Jahrhunderts*, AfMW 16 (1959), pp. 232-245; and Günther Schmidt, *Grundsätzliche Bemerkungen zur Geschichte der Passionshistorie*, AfMW 17 (1960), pp. 100-125.

There are three principal features by which the structures of the various surviving works are differentiated: these are (i) the extent to which polyphonic settings of text sections other than the crowd utterances are included; (ii) the extent to which the traditional plainsong Passion tones are used as *cantus firmi* to permeate the polyphonic texture; and (iii) the presence, in some Passions, of an Italianate, declamatory (*falsobordone*) style of writing which separates them stylistically from the main corpus of works. The overall range of techniques involved is in fact sufficiently wide to remove, in the intermediate stages, clear-cut distinctions between Kade's two basic categories, the Dramatic Passion characteristics being almost imperceptibly merged with those of the Motet Passion. At one end of the range there is the simplest Responsorial type of Passion in which only the crowd utterances (*turbae*) are set polyphonically, the traditional plainchant being retained for the narration and all the other sayings, and in which the so-called Passion tones are normally used as strict *cantus firmi* woven into the *turba* settings; examples of such are the Passions by Johann Walter, Guerrero (St Matthew and St John), Victoria (St Matthew and St John), Byrd and Lassus (St Mark and St Luke). At the other end of the scale there is the fully polyphonic, Motet type of Passion setting built up from successive, interlocked sections of imitative counterpoint and either quite free from, or only slightly influenced by, the traditional Passion tones; examples of these are found in the works of Gallus, Lechner and Demantius.

But between these two extremes a number of variant patterns exist. There are, for example, modifications of the basic Dramatic Passion scheme in which additional parts of the Gospel story are set polyphonically—sometimes the words of the minor characters only, sometimes also the words of Christ

—and in which much less strict use is made of the Passion tones as *cantus firmi*; in some cases the sayings of the individual characters are distinguished from those of the crowd by a reduction in the number of voice-parts, in others they are not. Then, again, there are other Passions, now described as 'Through-composed', which approach more nearly to the fully-fledged Motet setting. One type, an early type as exemplified in the works of Obrecht/Longaval, Resinarius and Galliculus, consists of continuous polyphonic settings of the entire narrative (frequently in an adapted or abbreviated form) in which the traditional plainsong basis is strictly retained and in which fairly clear-cut distinctions are made between the crowd utterances and those of the single characters by the disposition of the voice-parts. A further type of great interest comprises works which are again settings of the entire Gospel story (including all the words of narration) but which are set in clearly divided sections, often with a reduced number of voices for the individual characters, and with the narrative portions of the text presented in a sharply defined, *falsobordone* type of declamation; examples of these are the works by Cyprian de Rore, Giovanni Nasco, Vincenzo Ruffo and Ludovicus Daser.

A general outline of this rather complex pattern of structures may be set out as follows:

(A) *Responsorial Passions*
    (a) Only the *turba* choruses set polyphonically; Passion tones retained strictly as *cantus firmi*.
    (b) *Turba* choruses and the words of the minor characters (*not* the words of Christ) set polyphonically; either free from, or only lightly influenced by, the Passion tones.
        Sub-categories: (i) No differentiation in the number of voice-parts between the *turba* choruses and the character utterances.
        (ii) Character utterances differentiated by being set for fewer voices than the *turba* choruses.
    (c) *Turba* choruses, the minor-character utterances and the words of Christ all set polyphonically. Often only the part of Christ is set for a reduced number

of voices, the minor-character utterances and the *turba* choruses sharing the same vocal lay-out.

(B) *Through-Composed Passions*

    (a) Continuous polyphonic settings of the whole narrative; Passion tones used as strict *cantus firmi*.

    (b) Sectionalized polyphonic settings of the whole narrative, strongly influenced by Italian *falsobordone* technique; free introduction of Passion tones.

(C) *Motet Passions*

    Continuous polyphonic settings of the whole narrative, strongly influenced by motet style with interlocking sections of imitative counterpoint; normally free from the influence of Passion tones.

It is interesting to notice that, in the development of certain types of Passion structure, there was an elaborate pattern of cross-currents of influence between composers of different nationalities, the initial impetus coming frequently from Italy and later spreading northwards across Europe. Particularly striking is the fact that, whereas some Passion types seem at first to have been cultivated almost exclusively by native Italian composers others were fostered mainly by composers of northern European origin who had settled in Italy, frequently absorbing traits of style from their adopted country. For example the type of Responsorial Passion A(c), in which not only the *turbae* and the minor-character utterances, but also the words of Jesus, are set polyphonically, appears initially to have been composed solely by Italians and only to have spread northwards later in the century. On the other hand instances of Through-composed Passions by native Italians are extremely rare (only two examples, a St Matthew and a St John by Vincenzo Ruffo, have survived), type B(a) being developed mainly by northern and central European composers, such as Longaval and Resinarius, while type B(b) was particularly cultivated by expatriate northerners who were settled in Italy, such as Nasco and de Rore. Nasco's St Matthew and de Rore's St John are available in a modern edition by Arnold Schmitz (in *Musikalische Denkmäler*, Vol. 1, *Oberitalienische Figuralpassionen des 16. Jahrhunderts*, Mainz, 1955), the preface to which contains detailed historical and analytical notes on the music; this volume also includes St John Passions by Jaquet of Mantua and G. M. Asola. A further interesting distinction is found in the Responsorial type of Passion between the two sub-categories under A(b); the works in sub-category (i) were for the most part the products of native Italian composers whereas those in sub-category (ii) were almost exclusively by northerners.

The earliest known Responsorial Passions of type A(c), in which the words of Christ, as well as the *turbae* and the minor-character utterances, were composed in polyphony, are the three settings (one according to St Matthew, à 4, and two according to St John, à 4 and à 6, dating from before 1541) by the Italian, Gaspar de Albertis, who was choirmaster of the Santa Maria Maggiore church at Bergamo, where he died *c.* 1563. These works, which are preserved in two choirbooks in the music archives at Bergamo (Bergamo Codex 1207D and 1208D), are discussed in detail in an article by Knud Jeppesen: *A forgotten master of the early 16th century: Gaspar de Albertis*, Musical Quarterly 44 (1958), pp. 311-328. All three Passions are written for two choruses which, however, never sing together, one chorus (in Codex 1207D) presenting the *turbae* and the minor-character utterances, while the other (in Codex 1208D) sings only the words of Christ. The *Vox Christi* sections are set in all the Passions for a four-part chorus of men's voices, marked to be sung '*a voce mutata*', whereas the *turbae* and the sayings of the individual characters show rather more variety of treatment. In the six-part St John Passion, for example, the *turbae* are set for the full S.S.A.T.T.B. chorus, while the individuals are represented by smaller groups, Peter by an A.T.B. trio and the others by duos (e.g. Ancilla ostiara—two trebles; Pilate—tenor and bass). The example set by Gaspar de Albertis in these Passions was followed by a number of later Italian composers, such as P. Aretino, D. P. Falconio, G. M. Asola, C. D. Serafino and, in the early seventeenth century, F. Soriano, though in the later stages it became the established custom to set the part of Christ for a three-voice ensemble.

It is virtually certain that these settings by Albertis were known to Antonio Scandello and that it was he who transplanted this Passion type to Germany when he went there, *c.* 1550, to work as a member of the court chapel at Dresden. In Scandello's St John Passion (see O. Kade, op. cit. p. 190, and p. 306 where there is a complete transcription of the work) the part of Christ is set, as in Albertis, for a four-part choir, the minor characters being represented by smaller, duo and trio groups. A later German example of this structure is the St Mark Passion (1610) by Ambrosius Beber (modern edition by Simone Wallon in *Das Chorwerk* 66) which was clearly based on Scandello. It was Scandello who also achieved distinction as the first known composer of a *Resurrection History*, in which once again the part of Christ is set for a four-part ensemble; this tradition was undoubtedly handed on direct to Schütz (a successor of Scandello's at Dresden) who, in his *Resurrection History* (1623), again sets Christ's words for a small vocal group, in this case alto and tenor with *basso continuo*. It is tempting to conjecture that when Schütz, in the Preface to his *Resurrection History*, expressed his preference that in performance only the Evangelist should be visible, the other characters being hidden from view,[1] he may, perhaps unconsciously, have been echoing a tradition started nearly a century earlier by Gaspar de Albertis in Bergamo; it is not impossible that, when Albertis marked his *Vox Christi* choruses to be sung '*a voce mutata*', he too may have intended the 'changed' character of the singing to be achieved by some kind of concealment of the performers.

IV. THE AUTHORSHIP OF THE OBRECHT/LONGAVAL PASSION *(see page 26)*

The reasons why the attribution of the earliest 'Through-composed' Passion to Obrecht is probably mistaken are somewhat complex and are worth examining more closely. In the first printed version of the work, in *Selectae Harmoniae quatuor vocum de Passione Domini*, published by Georg Rhaw at Wittenburg in 1538, Obrecht is named as the composer; furthermore Obrecht's name is also given in a number of sixteenth-century middle-German manuscripts, the writers of which were presumably following Rhaw's ascription. But on the other hand there are two considerably earlier manuscripts of the work, now at Florence (Nat. Cent. II I 232) and at Rome (Vat. Cod. Sist. 42), neither of which mention

---

[1] 'Es were zwar noch viel zuerindern, auss was massen diese *Histori* mit besserer *gratia* oder anmuth *musiciret* werden köndte, wann nehmlich der Evangelist allein gesehen würde, die andern Personen alle verborgen stünden, und was mehr dergleichen ist'.

Obrecht but bear other ascriptions; in the Florence source the work is attributed to Longaval and in the Rome source to Jo(hannes) à la Venture. In his *Fausses attributions et travestissements musicaux* (Bulletin de la classe des beaux-arts de l'Académie Royale de Belgique, Brussels, 1941) Charles van den Borren indicates that la Venture is a French form of the Flemish name, Longaval or Longueval, from which we may infer that the attributions in the two Italian sources mentioned above are both to the same composer. It seems fairly certain that Longaval is the musician, Antoine de Longueval, who is known to have served at the court of the French kings Louis XII and Francis I from 1509 to 1523, being specifically named as *maître de premier chantre* in 1517. Beyond this very little indeed is known about his life or of the reasons why the manuscripts of his Passion should have been preserved in Italy.

In his detailed study of the authorship problem of the 'Obrecht' Passion (*De Matthaeus-Passie van Jacob Obrecht*, Tijdschrift der Vereeniging voor Nederlandsche Muziekgeschiedenis, XIV [1935], p. 182) Albert Smijers dates the two Italian manuscript sources as 'before 1507'. Acceptance of this early dating certainly gives principal authority to the two Italian sources and it seems reasonable, in the absence of further evidence, to accept Longaval as the composer. In addition some, more negative, support for the ascription to Longaval derives from the fact that, in Johann Walter's copy of the work in the great *Kantional* of 1545, the composer is not identified; if Obrecht had been the composer it seems likely that Walter would have known it and would have acknowledged it in his manuscript. By the time of Georg Rhaw's publication in 1538 Obrecht had been dead for thirty-three years and it is not difficult to imagine how confusion may have arisen to account for the mistaken attribution. Rhaw's published version differs in a number of details from the versions in the Italian manuscripts; in particular Rhaw's version gives '*secundum Matthaeum*' in all voices in the opening *Exordium* whereas the Italian sources give the names of all four Evangelists simultaneously in the four voice-parts.

Apart from its considerable intrinsic beauty the Obrecht/Longaval Passion is of outstanding interest as an archetypal work which was to exert a strong influence, both by its text and by its music, on succeeding generations of Passion composers. It is not known who the original compiler of the text was but his elegant and skilful 'harmonization' of the four Gospel accounts of the Passion formed the basis of nearly every later Through-composed Passion. In particular the final section with its presentation of all the last seven words from the Cross probably served as the model for Johann Bugenhagen's German compilation of the *Sieben Worte am Kreuz* which was set by a number of composers up to the time of Schütz. The extent of the musical influence of the Obrecht/Longaval Passion may be judged from the fact that adaptations of its *Introitus* chorus are to be found in some later Responsorial works such as Stephani's St Matthew Passion,[1] Besler's St Mark Passion and an anonymous Swedish St John Passion, dating probably from after 1570. The relationship between the opening chorus of Obrecht/Longaval and that of the Swedish Passion can be seen in Example 20.

This Swedish St John Passion is of considerable interest because it indicates the extent to which the vernacular had been adopted in Scandinavian countries during the late sixteenth and early seventeenth centuries. Musically the work is extremely simple, relying heavily upon the model of the German Passions attributed to Johann Walter and presenting, in primitive chordal responses, only the utterances of the crowd. Unlike the Walter Passions the Swedish work includes both *Introitus* and *Conclusio* choruses. The *Introitus* chorus, quoted in Example 20, appears to have been drawn

Example 20   (a) *Through-composed Passion* (pre-1507)

Obrecht/Longaval

(a)

---

[1] This setting is not an original composition by Stephani; not only is the *Introitus* adapted from Obrecht/Longaval but the main body of the work is borrowed directly from Johann Walter.

(b) *St John Passion* (post-1570) Anon. Swedish

most directly from that in Stephani's St Matthew Passion of 1570, which gives some clue to the probable dating of the Swedish work. The anonymous Swedish St John Passion is available in a modern edition in *Musica Svecica* XVII, 1, Stockholm, 1962, edited by Lennart Reimers.

V. AUGENMUSIK (EYE-MUSIC) *(see page 28)*

Augenmusik, music designed to appeal to the eye of the performer rather than the ear of the listener, is a device which was cultivated mainly by madrigalists during the sixteenth and early seventeenth centuries and is found only rarely in Passion music. There is, however, one interesting use of the device which is virtually confined to Passion composition because it hinges on the double meaning attached to the German word *Kreuz* (Latin: *crux*) whereby it may signify either a cross or the musical sharp sign. A number of cases can be found where references in the text to the Cross or to crucifixion are accompanied by sharps inserted into the vocal melodic lines, providing the performers with visible symbols of a basic Passion concept. As a general rule the application of sharps to the melodic lines at these places is contrived in such a way that the audible effect on the overall harmony and tonality within the musical context is relatively mild. A typical instance, where the visual effect is considerably more striking than the aural one, occurs in bar twenty of the third part of the St John Passion (1631) by Demantius; here the word '*kreuzigten*' is set to the chord of the dominant of A, involving a sharpening of the note G and a naturalizing (also indicated at this period by a sharp sign) of the B flat in the key signature. In bars thirty-one and thirty-two of the same part of the Passion a rather more colourful harmonic effect is achieved by setting the first syllable of the word '*Kreuze*' to an augmented triad with G sharp in the alto line and with a notationally unnecessary natural (i.e. sharp sign) placed against the note E in the first soprano part.

There is however a much more extravagant, and problematic, instance to be found in the eight-part St John Passion (1587) by Jacobus Gallus (Jacob Handl) where, in bars four and five of the third part, the word '*crucifigentibus*' gives rise to a plethora of sharps; these, if strictly applied, wrench the music violently from its basic tonal centre, producing a chord-progression which, by any normal standards of the period, is wildly unorthodox.[1]

[1] The example is given here as it is printed in *Denkmäler der Tonkunst in Österreich*, XII, 1, Vol. 24, *Jacob Handl (Gallus) Opus Musicum II*, p. 130, and in O. Kade, op. cit., p. 58.

Example 21   *St John Passion* (1587)   Jacob Handl (Gallus)

Nevertheless it is difficult to assert with any confidence that, in this case, the sharps are pure 'eye-music' and that they are not intended to be observed in practice. Complete omission of all the sharps gives a very colourless, neutral chord-progression, untypical of this usually adventurous composer; and it is interesting to notice that, though the actual chording at this point undoubtedly presents intonation problems, the individual vocal lines are not difficult to pitch, particularly if the second soprano E sharp is thought of as F natural and the first alto G sharp as A flat. It seems probable that this is an extreme case where the striking visual appearance of the music is intended to be combined with an even more astonishing aural effect (see A. Schmitz, *Zur motettischen Passion des 16. Jahrhunderts,* AfMW 16 [1959], p. 243; Schmitz gives a somewhat different interpretation of the accidentals).

The traditional use of the 'cross = sharp' symbolism was continued sporadically in later Passion compositions during the Baroque period and it is probably not without significance that, in the two famous *Lass ihn kreuzigen* (Let him be crucified) choruses in Bach's St Matthew Passion, the first syllable of '*kreuzigen*' is invariably set to a note which is inflected by a sharp sign.

In madrigal compositions, *Augenmusik* arises most frequently from the use of black notation in places where the text refers to 'grief', 'mourning', 'death', 'darkness', 'night' and so on, thus producing an obvious visual symbolism. The musical effect of black notation (filled notes) in a surrounding context of purely white notes (unfilled notes, such as breves, semibreves and minims) is to produce the rhythmic alteration known as *proportio sesquialtera* where three notes (a triplet formation) are fitted to the time of two. One of the earliest examples (a non-madrigalian example) of this type of *Augenmusik* occurs in the *Credo* of Ockeghem's *Missa Mi-Mi* (mid-fifteenth century) where the word '*mortuorum*' (of the dead) is set in black notation with clear symbolic intention. A much later English instance is to be found in the madrigal *Fusca, in thy starry eyes* by Thomas Tomkins (*c.* 1572-1656) where in the *tripla* section '*Love in black still mourning dies,* the word 'black' is set in black notation (see Denis Stevens, *Thomas Tomkins 1572-1656,* Dover, 1967, p. 114). Because of its association with death, grief and mourning it would not be surprising if this black-notation type of *Augenmusik* occurred fairly frequently in Passion music; yet to the present author's knowledge there is only one surviving instance. This occurs in the six-part St Matthew Passion by Johannes Herold which was composed at Klagenfurt in 1594 (see H. J. Moser, *Lutheran Composers in the Hapsburg Empire*, Musica Disciplina, Vol. 3, Fasc. 1, 1949, p. 15; a modern edition by H. J. Moser is available in *Musik älterer Meister*, Vol. 4, *Johannes Herold: Historia des Leidens und Sterbens unsers Herrn und Heilands*, Graz, 1955). In this work, during the scene of Jesus's betrayal by Judas, the 'blackness' of the traitor's deed is most aptly symbolized by a triplet figure, set in four-part choral harmony to the words '*Und küsset ihn*' (And kissed him), which is given visual expression by the characteristic black notation.

VI. THE ST MATTHEW PASSION ATTRIBUTED TO FRIEDRICH FUNCKE (*see page 92*)

There has recently come to light a further Passion from Lüneburg which clearly shows the influence of Christian Flor. This is an anonymous St Matthew Passion for solo voices and four-part choir, with an accompaniment for strings and *continuo*, the surviving source of which is preserved at Lüneburg (MS. Ratsbücherei Lüneburg, mus. ant. pract. KN. 201). In a detailed account of the work (*Eine unbekannte anonyme Matthaeuspassion aus der zweiten Hälfte des 17. Jahrhunderts*, AfMW XV (1958), pp. 162–186) Joachim Birke presents some cogent arguments to show that the composer was probably Friedrich Funcke (1642–1699). Of particular significance are the facts that (i) the Passion is linked in the source with a Litany known to be by Funcke, (ii) the manuscript of the Passion, which like that of the Litany appears to be in Funcke's handwriting, contains the expert, knowledgeable corrections one may expect from a composer rather than a scribe, (iii) a *symphonia* in the work is marked 'Lamento', an expression apparently only found in one other Lüneburg Passion, Funcke's setting, *c.* 1683, of St Luke's account (the manuscript of which was unfortunately lost during the Second World War), and (iv) the musical style of the Passion relates closely to that of a known work by Funcke, the *Danck- und Denck-Mahl* of

1666. A modern edition of this St Matthew Passion has been published by Joachim Birke in *Das Chorwerk* No. 78/79, Möseler Verlag, Wolfenbüttel, 1960. Its date of composition cannot at present be fixed more precisely than between 1667 and 1683, the dates of Flor's St Matthew and Funcke's St Luke settings respectively.

Funcke, who was born at Nossen in Saxony in 1642, became cantor at the St Johann church in Lüneburg in 1664, where he remained until 1694; his career thus coincided with that of Christian Flor who was organist of the church of St Lambert in Lüneburg from 1652 until his death in 1697, and who also doubled as organist at St Johann during the last twenty-one years of his life. It is very probable that, even during the earliest part of his career at Lüneburg, Funcke would have had close contact with Flor, since his duties as cantor at the St Johann church embraced responsibility for some of the choral performances at St Lambert; indeed it is quite likely that he may have assisted at the first performance of Flor's St Matthew in 1667.

In its general structure, and in the placing of its lyrical commentary, Funcke's St Matthew Passion (as we shall call the work from here on) follows the model of the Flor Passion very closely. In addition to the *Introitus* and *Conclusio* choruses there are twelve solo arias (of which four are repeats), nine *symphonias* and a motet in two *partes*. As in Flor's work the purely instrumental movements (which appear to have been a special feature of the Lüneburg Passions) are used mainly to break up, and comment upon, the extended scene of the Agony in the Garden, the interpolations being set in precisely the same contexts. The occasional repeats of arias result from the composer's selection of two particular chorales, the settings for solo voice of *O Lamm Gottes unschuldig* and *Christe du Lamm Gottes*, for placing at focal points in the drama. In the choice of these chorales, and of the contexts in which they are placed, Funcke again follows exactly the example of Flor. A further close parallel to Flor's scheme can be seen in Funcke's treatment of the meditation on the scene of the death of Jesus, where the two *partes* of a motet, probably the traditional *Ecce quomodo moritur justus*, are separated by an instrumental *symphonia* and followed by an alto aria, *Ist dieser nicht des Höchsten Sohn?*, based on a text by Johann Rist (cf. pp. 91-92). It is interesting to notice that, in the original choir-books, no text or music is given at the point where the motet occurs, but simply an *incipit*, either '*Siehe*' or '*Ecce*', followed by the word '*tacet*', suggesting the possibility that a second choir, in another part of the church, may have sung the special music at this point. The fact that in some of the choir-books the *incipit* is given in German points to the further likelihood that a special German version of the motet (perhaps by Funcke) may occasionally have been performed in place of the famous Latin one by Jacobus Gallus. The longest, and most impressive, section of meditative commentary in the work is a setting for solo soprano and strings of the chorale verse, *Erbarm dich mein, o Herre Gott* (No. 22 in the score), which occupies a central position in the work, as a meditation on the scene of Peter's denial. This is a movement of great beauty, a finely wrought chorale prelude on a melody originally composed by Johann Walter (*Geystliche gesangk Buchleyn*, 1524); the texture consists of five real parts, the voice contributing one strand in equal partnership with the strings. At the opening the chorale melody (in a paraphrased version, with rising chromatic steps) is presented initially by the first violins, while the voice and the lower strings contribute expressive counterthemes; later the voice takes up the principal melody, still in a paraphrased form, and against it the orchestra weaves an elaborate web of counterpoint. Here again, in his choice of the chorale verse and his placing of it in the Passion framework, Funcke was clearly influenced by Flor, and also contributed thereby to a tradition which (as we have seen earlier on p. 91) was later transmitted to Bach.

Where the Funcke Passion differs most markedly from Flor's is in the setting of the Evangelist's narration and of the words of the single characters, including Christ. In Flor's Passion all these sections of the account are set to be sung, quite unaccompanied, to a form of mock-plainsong, largely borrowed from an earlier work—Melchior Vulpius's setting, 1613, of St Matthew (cf. p. 37). Funcke, on the other hand, adopts a different, possibly even earlier, mock-plainsong version and provides it with a strange, rather clumsy, accompaniment for the instrumental *basso continuo*, recalling the procedure found in Thomas Selle's second St John Passion (see p. 51). The transitional character of Funcke's work is here clearly demonstrated; no doubt he felt that the ancient, unaccompanied plainsong style was inappropriate in a work which contained many new, even revolutionary features, and yet he lacked the experience and technical resource to supply a fully operatic type of setting. His compromise solution is not very satisfactory, showing neither the flexibility of pure plainsong nor the 'natural' fluency of recitative.

By contrast with the somewhat rudimentary style of these narrative settings the *turba* choruses are composed with considerable technical skill, allied to a fine sense of drama and apt characterization. Many of these sections contain several contrasted musical ideas, with interchanges of triple and quadruple time and clearly differentiated indications of speed. A notable example occurs in the final *turba* chorus of the Passion (No. 45 in the score), *Herr, wir haben gedacht, dass dieser Verführer sprach . . .* (Sir, we remember that that deceiver said . . .). Here, after a four-bar homophonic opening with a lively orchestral accompaniment, the chorus freely declaim (in bare octaves and without instrumental support) the saying of the 'deceiver'—*Ich will nach dreien Tagen wieder auferstehen'* (After three days I will rise again). Then the changing moods of the remainder of the text are portrayed in continuous music by successive alterations of time and speed, as follows : (i) *Allegro*, quadruple time, *'Darum befiehle dass man das Grab verwahre . . .'* (Command therefore that the sepulchre be made sure . . .), (ii) *Presto*, triple time, *'Er ist auferstanden'* (He is risen), (iii) *Adagio*, quadruple time, *'von den Toten'* (from the dead), and (iv) *Allegro*, quadruple time, *'und werde der letze Betrug . . .'* (so that the last error shall be worse than the first). A further striking instance of the rich variety of Funcke's scheme is shown by the two 'Crucify' choruses. The first of these (No. 26 in the score) is a massive homophonic passage, marked *Adagio* and in quadruple time, which creates the impression of a solemn and carefully weighed judgment; but immediately afterwards, when the mob reiterate their demand, they do so at an *Allegro* speed, in triple time, with dotted rhythms and closely spaced imitative entries, revealing now the frenzy and hysteria by which they are truly motivated.

Lüneburg was clearly an important centre for the development of Passion music; in addition to Flor's early, pioneer setting and the anonymous Passion under discussion, two later works of historical interest are known to have been composed there: Funcke's St Luke Passion (c. 1683), in which the part of Christ was daringly rewritten in rhymed paraphrase, and a further setting of St Luke (1711) by Georg Böhm. Unfortunately only the libretti of these works have survived, the music being lost. The rediscovery of the St Matthew Passion attributed to Funcke has supplied some valuable additional evidence of the way in which the ancient Dramatic Passion gradually evolved into the Passion Oratorio. Although the composer clearly relied heavily for his structure on the pattern established by Flor, and achieved only modest success in his experimentation with the narrative-setting, he nevertheless showed a significant growth in technical resource, particularly in his treatment of the *symphonias*, arias and *turba* choruses, and in his ability to sustain interest over a musical canvas of increased size.

VII. JOHANN MEDER'S ST MATTHEW PASSION, C. 1700
(see page 83)

In view of the considerable importance of Meder's Passion Oratorio[1] in the history of the genre, and its limited accessibility at the present time, it will be useful to record here some straightforward factual details of the work's scoring and structure. The setting is for five-part chorus (S.S.A.T.B.) with an orchestra consisting of two flutes (probably recorders), two oboes, two violins, two viols (*viole* and *violette*) and *basso continuo*; the main key is F major. The individual characters are represented by solo voices as follows: Evangelist (tenor), Jesus (bass), Judas (alto), Peter (tenor), the false witnesses (alto and tenor), Caiaphas (bass), Maid (soprano), Pilate (bass) and Pilate's wife (soprano). The words of the Evangelist and of all the minor characters are accompanied by *continuo* alone, whereas the sayings of Jesus have an additional accompaniment for two violins, the parts being, in some places, marked *tremolo*. The arias are accompanied variously by flute, oboe, violins and viols (with *continuo*), singly and in combination. Precise details of the orchestration are not

---

[1] Johann Valentin Meder, *Passions-Oratorium nach dem Evangelisten Matthaeus*, Deutsche Bibliothek Berlin Mus. MS., an autograph MS. of the period. The present writer's knowledge of the work is based on a handwritten copy kindly lent by Miss Patience Robertson.

always given; for example, at the opening of the work, where, after an eleven-bar *symphonia*, the chorus sings the introductory words, '*Höret das Leiden und Sterben unsers Herren Jesu Christi . . .*', the only indication of instrumental support is that given by the rubric, '*instrumenta concordant cum cantantibus*'; it seems likely that the orchestra is also intended to join in with the voices in many of the succeeding *turba* choruses and very probably in the final *Danksagungslied*, which is written in a massive, triple-time homophonic style, using the text (as in Vulpius, Flor, Funcke and others) '*Dank sei unser Herren Jesu Christi, der uns erlöset hat . . .*'.

The Passion is remarkably rich in meditative commentary, consisting of twenty short movements in the form of arias, duets, chorales and instrumental *symphonias*; frequently the arias are based on chorale texts and (as in the Lüneburg Passions; see Appendix VI) on paraphrased versions of chorale melodies. It should be noticed, however, that several of these reflective movements appear to be later additions to the original manuscript, being either pasted into the score or added in different ink. The details of the sections of meditative commentary, and of their contexts in the narrative, are as follows :

   (i) After Jesus's words, '*Nehmet, esset, das ist mein Leib*', ARIA, *Herr, Jesu Christe . . .*, with accompaniment for flute, two violins and *continuo*, the voice-part marked '*Canto nel Tenore*'.

   (ii) After Jesus's words, '*. . . wird für viele zur Vergebung der Sünden*', ARIA (v. 4 of the preceding aria) for voice and *continuo* only.

   (iii) After Jesus's words, '*. . werde mit euch in meines Vaters Reich*', DUET, *Das Blut Jesu Christi*, for two sopranos (or tenors) and *continuo*. This duet is pasted into the score.

   (iv) After Jesus's words, '*. . . bis dass ich dorthin gehe und bete*', SYMPHONIA for two flutes and *continuo* in C minor.

   (v) After Jesus's words, '*. . . doch nicht wie ich will, sondern wie du willst*', SYMPHONIA for flute, two violins and *continuo* in E flat major.

   (vi) After Jesus's words, '*. . . ich trinke ihn denn, so geschehe dein Wille*', SYMPHONIA, very similar to the preceding but only half as long.

(vii) After Jesus's words, *'wie würde aber die Schrift erfüllet? Es muss also gehen'*, SYMPHONIA for two oboes, two violins and *continuo*, containing answering phrases between the oboes and violins.

(viii) After the crowd chorus, *'Er ist des Todes schuldig'*:
    (1) SYMPHONIA—the same as the preceding *symphonia*.
    (2) CHORALE, *O Lamm Gottes unschuldig*, a single melodic line with a figured *continuo* bass—in G major—verse 1. This chorale appears to be pasted in; the handwriting is the same as the rest of the MS., but the ink is different.

(ix) After the narration, *'. . . und ging hinaus und weinete bitterlich'*, SYMPHONIA for two oboes, two violins and *continuo*.

(x) After the crowd chorus, *Sein Blut komme über uns und über unsre Kinder*, CHORALE, *O Lamm Gottes*—in G major—verse 2.

(xi) After the narration, *'. . . dass er gekreuziget würde'*, CHORALE, *O Lamm Gottes*—in G major—verse 3. Pasted into the MS.

(xii) After the crowd chorus, *Gegrüsset seist du, der Juden König*, an indication of interpolations in the MS., no text or music given.

(xiii) After the narration, *'. . . dass er ihm sein Kreuze trug'*, ARIA, *Christe du Lamm Gottes*, for soprano with oboe, two viols (with alto and tenor clefs) and *continuo*.

(xiv) After the crowd chorus, *Der du den Tempel Gottes zerbrichst . . .*, the words, *'Christe du Lamm Gottes'*, in the MS.; no music. Probably a repeat of the previous aria is intended.

(xv) After the narration, *'. . . die mit ihm gekreuziget waren'*, CHORALE, *O Lamm Gottes*, a four-part (S.A.T.B.) setting, marked *'per tutto choro'*.

(xvi) After the crowd chorus, *Er rufet den Elias*, ARIA, *Christe du Lamm Gottes*, as before; this aria is written in with different ink from the rest of the M.S.

(xvii) After the crowd chorus, *Halt, lass sehen ob Elias komme und ihm helfe*:
    (1) SYMPHONIA, marked *'Preludio'*, for oboe, two violins and *continuo*—in B flat major; pasted into the MS.
    (2) ARIA, *Christe du Lamm Gottes*, the setting identical with (xiii) above.

(xviii) After the narration of the death of Jesus, '... *aber Jesus schreit laut und verschied*', ARIA (possibly based on a chorale) in F major, with four verses set as follows: (1) soprano solo, (2) tutti, (3) tenor solo, (4) tutti.

(xix) After the narration: '... *für die Tür des Grabes und ging davon*':

    (1) SYMPHONIA for oboe, two violins and *continuo*—in G minor.

    (2) CHORALE, *O Traurigkeit, O Herzeleid*, and elaborate setting as follows: (a) soprano solo with two *violette* and *continuo*, (b) tenor solo with two oboes and *continuo*, (c) chorus (S.A.T.B.) with oboe and *continuo*, (d) solo voices (S.T.B.) with *continuo* (a florid quaver bass in 12/8 time), (e) chorus (S.A.T.B.) with two oboes, two violins and *continuo*; the oboes double the melody while the violins supply decorative parts in quavers.

It will be seen from a comparison between the foregoing and the information in Appendix VI that Meder (or whoever made the later additions in the manuscript) has placed his meditative commentary in accordance with the plan established by the Lüneburg composers, Christian Flor and Friedrich Funcke, choosing for the most part the same texts and the same chorale melodies where these are used. Like these earlier composers Meder splits up the lengthy dialogue scenes of the Last Supper and the Agony in the Garden at Gethsemane, selecting much the same places for his interpolations; Meder, however, introduces during these scenes only seven movements (two arias, a duet and four *symphonias*) as compared with Flor's twelve movements (four arias and eight *symphonias*) and Funcke's eleven movements (three arias and eight *symphonias*). The most striking respect in which Meder departs from normal tradition is by apparently omitting the customary motet, *Ecce quomodo moritur justus*, after the scene of the death of Christ, replacing it by a ten-bar strophic aria in F major, the four verses of which have varied settings.

The *turba* choruses are all for five-part (S.S.A.T.B.) choir and frequently display the use of a partly homophonic and partly imitative or melismatic style of writing. Very often the composer seems to be seeking to create a strong dramatic impact by setting the opening phrase of a chorus in a massively chordal style, thereafter allowing the music to become more florid. An instance of this kind of treatment can be seen in Example 22, the utterance of the crowd during the hearing before Caiaphas, *'Er ist des Todes schuldig'* (He is guilty of death).

The words of the Evangelist and of the minor characters are set in a purely operatic *recitativo secco* style, which is flexible, carefully 'punctuated' by rests and sensitively mated with the text; no doubt Meder's experience in the theatre, in such works as the opera *Nero* (1695) composed for performance at Danzig, served him well here. The sayings of Christ, on the other hand, are written in a more restrained *arioso* style, this technique being of course largely dictated by the presence of the accompanying violins. The creation of a clear distinction between the operatic *recitativo* style of the Evangelist's part and the smoother *arioso* manner of Christ's role interestingly foreshadows the method used later by Bach in his St Matthew Passion. Meder's examples of triple-time *arioso* are generally

Example 22   *St Matthew Passion (c. 1700)*   J. Meder

rather undistinguished, a typical instance being the trite, repetitive setting of the words instituting the Holy Communion, '*Nehmet, esset, das ist mein Leib*'; quadruple time, on the other hand, can stimulate him to a simple, yet dignified, manner, as is shown in Example 23. The exact method of interpreting the string *tremolo* is not known, but it almost certainly involved some rapid repetition of notes within the written rhythmic pattern.

There are some simple, but not ineffective, instances of word-painting; apart from the vocal *trillo* on the word '*erbebete*' (quaked), which is quoted in Example 16*b* on page 114, there are some rapid descending scales to symbolize 'fiel *auf sein Angesichte*' (fell on his face), '*da verliessen ihn alle Junger und* flohen' (then all the disciples forsook him and *fled*); on the other hand, '*zereiss in zwei Stück*' (rent in twain) and the crowing of the cock prompt rapid *ascending* scales, the ornamentation in the latter case being attached, rather unusually, to the word '*Hahn*' (cock) and not to the word '*krähet*' (crew).

Born at Wassungen (Werra) in 1649, Johann Valentin Meder

Example 23   *St Matthew Passion (c. 1700)*   J. Meder

was the youngest of the five sons of the Wassungen cantor, Johann Erhard Meder. During his early life he studied theology at Leipzig and Jena, later turning to music and travelling extensively (even as far as Copenhagen) as a singer and opera composer. A visit to Lübeck in 1674 brought him in contact with Buxtehude, whose influence on the style of the younger man's music can be clearly seen. Meder's St Matthew Passion, which was composed *c.* 1700, may have been written either at Danzig or, more probably, at Riga; early in 1700 he was appointed cantor to the cathedral in Danzig, but before the end of the year he relinquished this post in favour of a similar one as choir director at Riga cathedral, where he remained until his death in 1719. In addition to the Passion he composed at least three operas and a considerable quantity of occasional church music, much of which is now lost.

VIII. CHROMATICISM AND WORD-PAINTING *(see page 72)*

It is probably a mistake to suppose that, in his use of chromaticism for the purposes of word-painting, Bach was guided mainly by literary considerations. In many of the vocal works chromatic themes are, of course, prompted by single emotive words, such as 'death', 'fear' or 'grief', and sections of chromatic harmony coincide with expressive, colourful passages in the texts; but, as comparison with the purely instrumental works plainly shows, the laws governing the use of such chromaticism are primarily musical rather than literary. This point is clearly illustrated in an interesting article by Roger Bullivant (*Word-painting and chromaticism in the music of J. S. Bach*, The Music Review, 20 [1959], pp. 185-216) in which three principal types of chromaticism—thematic, sequential and preparatory—are defined and impressive evidence is assembled to show that Bach's motives for incorporating them both in his instrumental and vocal works were mainly musical ones. An interesting case is presented by the highly chromatic chorus from the St John Passion, *Wäre dieser nicht ein Übeltäter*, which shows a typical instance of the use of 'thematic' chromaticism. It is a mistake to think that, in this chorus, it was Bach's intention to create an overall picture of the crowd's fanaticism by means of harsh, 'advanced' harmony; this type of literary illustration formed no part of the composer's normal aesthetic system. The colourful effect of the opening of this chorus arises simply from the presence of a single chromatically ascending theme, set to the word *'Übeltäter'* (malefactor). Successive entries of this chromatic theme in the various voice-parts eventually produce a total permeation of the texture with chromaticism, but this only continues so long as the emotive word is still present; in the later part of the chorus, when presumably the crowd is still equally fanatical, chromaticism disappears because of the absence of the significant word. Similarly in the succeeding chorus, *Wir dürfen niemand töten*, chromaticism is prompted by the word '*töten*' (put to death), set to the same ascending theme. Apart from these two choruses there is surprisingly little use of chromaticism in Bach's settings of the crowd utterances, other means being found to achieve the appropriate expression. The '*kreuzige*' (crucify) choruses illustrate two typical methods of securing dramatic tension; in the St John Passion by the use of sharply dissonant suspensions between the various voice-parts, and in the St Matthew Passion by means of closely spaced entries of a modulating fugal theme which, though strangely twisted in shape, is non-chromatic.

Another interesting, and not uncommon, feature of word-painting in Baroque music is the device whereby a word's meaning is given expressive musical colouring despite the presence of a negative or some other means of cancelling its sense-implication within the whole context; this may be described as 'immediate' word-painting. To take an example at random, in Purcell's verse anthem *My Beloved Spake* the word 'winter' is painted musically by a gloomy passage in F minor without regard to the sense of the whole passage which in fact tells of *gladness* because winter has ended ('For lo, the winter is past, the rain is over and gone; the flowers appear upon the earth, and the time of the singing of birds is come.'). This 'immediate' type of word-painting occurs quite frequently in Bach and provides the reason for the apparent discrepancy, noted above, in the chorale-setting, *Er nahm Alles wohl in Acht*, St John Passion, No. 56 (see Example 12, p. 84). In this case the single word '*stirb*' (die) is painted symbolically by the use of colourful harmony without regard to the comforting context in which it is placed: '*stirb daraus* ohn' *alles Leid*' (die therefore *without* distress).

IX. J. S. BACH'S ST MARK PASSION *(see page 14)*

In recent years, following the lead given by Wilhelm Rust (in *Bachgesellschaft*, 20 [2], p. ix and the subsequent researches of Arnold Schering (*Bach-Jahrbuch* 36 [1939], pp. 1-32) and Friedrich Smend (*Bach-Jahrbuch* 37 [1940-48], pp. 1-35), an attempt has been made by D. Hellmann to reconstruct J. S. Bach's settings of some of the lyrical portions written by Picander for the Passion according to St Mark (1731).

Picander's libretto (published in *Ernst-Scherzhaffte und Satyrische Gedichte*, Vol. 3, Leipzig, 1732, p. 49) provides verses for the opening and final choruses, and for six arias. As early as 1873 Wilhelm Rust had pointed out that the texts of these two choruses and of three of the arias—*Mein Heiland, dich vergess ich nicht; Er kommt, er kommt, er ist vorhanden;* and *Mein Tröster ist nicht mehr bei mir*—corresponded exactly in metre and prosody to some of the texts which Picander had written for the Eberhardine *Trauer-Ode* of 1727, and that it was practically certain that Bach had 'borrowed' the related music of the earlier work when he came to compose the St Mark Passion. The remaining three arias presented a more difficult problem; some skilful detective work by Friedrich Smend revealed, however, that the alto aria *Falsche Welt, dein schmeichelnd Küssen* corresponded very closely, not only in metre but also in emotional expression, with the opening alto aria, *Widerstehe doch der Sünde*, from church cantata No. 54. A second aria, *Welt und Himmel, nehmt zu Ohren*, was found by Smend to relate fairly closely in metre to the aria, *Merkt und hört, ihr Menschenkinder*, from church cantata No. 7 (*Christ, unser Herr, zum Jordan kam*) but he rightly rejected this solution because of the wide discrepancy in the emotional expression underlying the two arias. Since then, however, D. Hellmann has shown that a more satisfactory, though by no means indisputably authentic, solution can be achieved by adapting the music of the soprano aria *Leit', o Gott, durch deine Liebe* (no. 3 from church cantata No. 120a. *Herr Gott, Beherrscher aller Dinge*) to this section of the Picander text. For the remaining aria, *Angenehmes Mordgeschrei*, no adaptable music has been found.

The text lay-out of the St Mark Passion (given in detail in W. Schmieder, *Thematisch-systematisches Verzeichnis der Werke Joh. Seb. Bachs*, Leipzig, 1950, pp. 363-365) shows that a remarkably generous provision was made for congregational chorales, of which there were sixteen in all, eight in each of the two parts of the work. Music for these chorales can be found with relatively little difficulty; the main source is the four sets of four-part chorale harmonizations by J. S. Bach which were published by his son, C. P. E. Bach, between 1784 and 1787. A number of these chorale-settings are from the well-known, fully-authenticated cantatas and Passions and it seems safe to assume that many of the others are probably from equally great works which are now lost, such as the St Mark Passion. In Smend's article (*Bach-Jahrbuch*, 1940-48) a list of the chorales in the lost Passion, together with details of the music which was probably associated with them, is set out on pages 9 to 12.

Hellmann's reconstruction of the lyrical sections of the St Mark Passion led, in 1964, to a performance in the church of St Goar, near Mainz-am-Rhein. Since then a gramophone recording of the work has been issued (Erato LDE 3346) which presents, in a well-organized sequence of meditative commentary, an extended type of Passion cantata, consisting of the opening and final choruses, the five 'restored' arias and five of the chorales. The music is of the very highest quality, noble and inspired, and well adapted to the text; but what is, of course, still lacking is the entire musical setting of the Gospel narrative, of the words of Christ and the other characters, and of the crowd utterances, without which the work must inevitably remain a mere shadow of the original conception. Many years ago Gerhard Freiesleben pointed out (in *Neue Zeitschrift für Musik*, Jahrg. 83, 1916, p. 237) that the music for the chorus *Pfui dich, wie fein zerbrichst du den Tempel* was in all probability later adapted by Bach for the chorus setting *Wo ist der neugeborne König* in the *Christmas Oratorio* (1734); but this single *turba* chorus can clearly have little practical effect without an extended musical context in which to place it.

The sequence of items on the gramophone recording is as follows:

Part I

1. CHORUS: *Geh, Jesu, geh zu deiner Pein!* — from *Trauer-Ode* No. 1, opening chorus, *Lass, Fürstin, lass noch einen Strahl*

2. ARIA (alto solo): *Mein Heiland, dich vergess ich nicht* (Context: after the Institution of the Holy Communion) — from *Trauer-Ode* No. 5, aria (alto solo), *Wie starb die Heldin so vergnügt*

3. CHORALE: *Betrübtes Herz, sei wohlgemut* (Context: 'My soul is exceeding sorrowful . . .') — melody: *Wenn mein Stündlein vorhanden ist*

157

4. ARIA (soprano solo): *Er kommt, er kommt, er ist vorhanden* (Context: '... lo! he that betrayeth me is at hand)

from *Trauer-Ode* No. 3, aria (soprano solo), *Verstummt, verstummt, ihr holden Saiten*

5. CHORALE: *Jesu, ohne Missetat* (Context: 'Are ye come out as against a thief? ...')

melody: *Jesu, der du selbsten wohl*

6. ARIA (alto solo): *Falsche Welt, dein schmeichelnd Küssen* (Context: '... Master, master and kissed him')

from cantata No. 54, aria (alto solo), *Widerstehe doch der Sünde*

7. CHORALE: *Ich will hier bei dir stehen* (Context: '... and they all forsook him and fled')

melody: *Herzlich tut mich verlangen*

Part II

8. ARIA (tenor solo): *Mein Tröster ist nicht mehr bei mir*

from *Trauer-Ode* No. 8, aria (tenor solo), *Der Ewigkeit saphirnes Haus zieht*

9. CHORALE: *Man hat dich sehr hart verhöhnet* (Context: 'And they smote him on the head with a reed ...')

melody: *Jesu, der du meine Seele*

10. ARIA (soprano solo): *Welt und Himmel, nehmt zu Ohren* (Context: '... and Jesus cried with a loud voice and gave up the ghost')

from cantata No. 120a, aria (soprano solo), *Leit', o Gott, durch deine Liebe*

11. CHORALE: *O! Jesu du, mein Hilf und Ruh!* (Context: 'There were also women looking on afar off ...')

melody: *O Traurigkeit*

12. CHORUS: *Bei deinem Grab und Leichenstein*

from *Trauer-Ode* No. 10, final chorus, *Doch, Königin! du stirbest nicht*

(It should be noted that the context order of items 5 and 6 is transposed in order to avoid consecutive arias and chorales at the end of Part I.)

Attention is drawn to the rich and unusual scoring of the items taken from the Eberhardine *Trauer-Ode*, the orchestra for which consists of two flauti traversi, two oboi d'amore, strings (including parts for two viole da gamba), two lutes and *continuo*. Particularly striking is the alto aria *Mein Heiland*, in which the voice is accompanied by the two viole da gamba, lutes and *continuo*.

X. THE PASSIONS OF G. P. TELEMANN (*see page 97*)

Telemann was the most prolific of all Passion composers; he is known to have written no less than forty-six liturgical Passions of which twenty now survive (up till 1945 twenty-three were extant, but the dispersal of manuscripts during the Second World War has apparently resulted in the loss of three further works).[1] Such source material (libretti and music) as now remains is preserved in the Hamburg State Archives and in the German State Library, Berlin. The long series of liturgical Passions was composed for Hamburg where, from 1721 until his death in 1767, Telemann was director of music at the St Johannes church and also at five other main churches in the city. One of his important duties as a church composer was to write an annual Passion setting; and so in each of the forty-six years of his tenure of office a new Passion was produced, apparently without any repetition of poetic texts or music over the whole period. This strong tradition for the annual production of an entirely new Passion appears to have been peculiar to Hamburg (where, indeed, the Oratorio Passion may be said to have originated with the work of Thomas Selle), and was not paralleled in other large cities like Leipzig; Bach's probable total output of only four Passions seems really quite modest when set beside the prodigious and ceaseless productivity of Telemann. Rather remarkably all the Hamburg Passion libretti have survived in an unbroken series from

---

[1] See the preface to the modern edition by H. Hörner and M. Ruhnke of the St Luke Passion (1728) in Vol. XV of *Georg Philipp Telemann, Musikalische Werke*, Bärenreiter, Kassel and Basel, 1964.

the year 1676 right through the late Baroque period and beyond; it is interesting to notice that during the 1690s a pattern was established whereby a regular sequence of settings of all the four Evangelists, Matthew, Mark, Luke and John, was presented in recurring four-year cycles. Telemann's first contribution was a St Matthew in 1722 and his last a setting of St Mark in 1767, the final year of his life.[1] After Telemann's death his Passion-music tradition is known to have been continued by his grandson, Georg Michael Telemann, who, while working in Riga between 1776 and 1827, gave twenty-one performances of his grandfather's compositions in this form. That so many of these Passions have been preserved today is in large measure due to the younger man's enthusiasm and affection for his ancestor's work.

In addition to his liturgical Passions Telemann also composed a considerable number of 'Opera' Passions designed for presentation outside church, usually in one of the city's theatres which were not available for normal dramatic productions during Lent. Typical of these works are the settings of Barthold Heinrich Brockes's *Der ... gemarterte und sterbende Jesus*, J. J. D. Zimmerman's *Betrachtung der neunten Stunden an dem Todestage Jesu*, and Ramler's *Tod Jesu*. Other librettists with whom Telemann collaborated were Hunold-Menantes, J. U. König, Postel (also the librettist of Handel's St John), Samuel Müller and M. A. Wilkens.

Telemann's Passion settings have long remained in obscurity, despite the valuable research in modern times by Hans Hörner *(G. P. Telemanns Passionsmusiken*, diss. Kiel, pub. Leipzig, 1933); possibly the sheer quantity of the works has been thought to be irreconcilable with quality. But recently the publication of modern editions of a few of the Passions, together with the issue of some gramophone recordings, has provided a welcome opportunity for a reassessment; and there can be no doubt that, as a result, Telemann's reputation has been considerably enhanced. The works now available are the St Luke Passion of 1728 (in Vol. XV of *Georg Philipp*

---

[1] A simple calculation from one of these known dates shows that 1705 was Hamburg's year for St John's account, which suggests (but by no means proves) that this, rather than 1704, may have been the year of the production of Handel's St John. Handel's authorship of this work is, however, now seriously questioned, Georg Böhm being considered a stronger claimant. Detailed evidence is yet to be published.

Telemann, Musikalische Werke, Bärenreiter, Kassel and Basel, 1964, edited by H. Hörner and M. Ruhnke), the St Matthew Passion of 1730 (piano score and orchestral parts, edited by Kurt Redel, published by Barocco Verlag, Vaduz [Liechtenstein], 1964; gramophone recording, Philips A 02489/90 L and 835 359/60 AY, stereo), and the St Mark Passion of 1759 (gramophone recording, Philips A 02351/52 L and 835 229/30 AY, stereo).

Each of these three settings is in its different way a work of considerable power and originality, rather more lightweight than Bach, as might be expected, but containing music of expressive substance far beyond the mere fluency and surface attractiveness so often associated with this composer. The three Passions differ considerably in structure. The work which corresponds most closely in design to the familiar Bach pattern is the St Matthew Passion (1730) in which the entire Gospel account of the Passion (Matthew, chap. 26 and chap. 27 to the end of v. 60) is set in the typical oratorio style, with a carefully balanced proportion of meditative commentary— arias, *arioso* settings, chorales, a duet and a commentary-chorus. The placing of the reflective material is, indeed, modelled quite closely on the traditional scheme which Bach himself adopted from the earlier Oratorio Passion composers, the most striking difference (both in Bach and Telemann) being the absence of the normal emotional reaction after the crowd's utterance *'Er ist des Todes schuldig'* (He is guilty of death). Telemann's setting of the words of the minor characters in the drama is rather unusual; in the St Matthew Passion (1730) these sections are invariably composed in a tuneful *arioso* style with measured melodic patterns (symmetrical and often sequential) set over bass-lines which imply regularity of harmonic rhythm. It is particularly noticeable that the part of Judas has a jolly, almost popular, flavour about it, as if the composer's intention was to portray him as a crude, insensitive character rather than as a sinister one. Within Telemann's frame of reference, which is overtly more operatic than Bach's, this type of characterization is not ineffective; but the somewhat studied triviality of the part of Judas, and to a lesser extent the rôles of Peter and Pilate, tends to diminish the artistic stature of the work, introducing an excessively theatrical element.

The St Mark Passion (1759) reveals a rather different structure because there is a heavier emphasis on reflective commentary; in particular the number of solo arias and chorales is considerably greater, with a consequent tendency for the Gospel narrative to become overshadowed. In order to accommodate this growth in the meditative element Telemann, or his unknown librettist, excluded entirely the Gospel scenes of the Last Supper and the Entombment, producing thereby a modified type of liturgical Passion—colourful, operatic and doubtless well-suited to contemporary taste. In this later work Telemann does not use measured *arioso* for the sayings of the minor characters but sets them very effectively in a free type of operatic *recitativo secco*. Christ's words are usually accompanied by *continuo* alone, though a 'halo' of string sound is added for some of the more impressive utterances, such as prophecies; the amount of this accompaniment is, however, very slight and its absence during the cry from the Cross, '*Eli, Eli, lama asabthani?*' seems to have no clear symbolic significance as it obviously does in Bach's St Matthew Passion (see pp. 51-52). The orchestra is fairly small (as in all Telemann's Passions), consisting of flutes (including piccolo), oboes (including the alto and tenor sizes), bassoon, strings and *continuo*, but it is used with great imaginativeness and a fine sense of colour.[1] Attention may be called to the vividly descriptive orchestral passage in rapid semiquavers which follows the Evangelist's account of the flight of the disciples from the place of Jesus's arrest; this links on directly to a passage of recitative, '*Ihr fliehet! Ach wo bleibt der Mut der kühnlich mit Jesu zu erblassen*', in which the baritone soloist vigorously reproaches the disciples for their faithlessness, the original 'flight' motif continuing to permeate the orchestral accompaniment.

The work which displays the most strikingly unusual construction is the St Luke Passion of 1728. In this setting the

---

[1] In the recording (mentioned above on p. 161) of the St Matthew Passion (1730) there is an expressive opening *sinfonia* for orchestra which, apart from some minor details of instrumentation, is identical with a programmatic movement entitled *Sommeille* (sic) from an *Ouverture* in C major also by Telemann. This *sinfonia* does not, however, appear in the original manuscript of the Passion; it has been specially added for this recorded performance. The *Ouverture*, together with some of Telemann's other orchestral works, has been recorded by the Saar Chamber Orchestra under Karl Ristenpart as an issue (now deleted) of the former Record Society: RS 64 (RSS 17).

Gospel narrative of the Passion is presented in five separate *partes* which are preceded by lengthy preparatory scenes from the Old Testament, each establishing clear typological relationships in the strict theological sense. Thus, at the very opening of the work, there is an extended musical scene (based on Genesis 37) depicting Joseph, sold by his brethren into captivity in Egypt; this prepares for, and relates to, the Passion scene of Jesus's betrayal by Judas and his desertion by his disciples.[1] In the presentation of the remainder of the Passion story similar Old Testament parallels are drawn as follows: the beating and mockery of the guiltless Christ before the High Priest is prepared by a scene (based on I Kings 22 and 2 Chronicles 18) showing the guiltless Micah, struck and reviled by Zedekiah for his divinely inspired, but unfavourable, prophecy on the impending fate of Ahab; Christ's condemnation before Pilate is prepared by a scene (based on 2 Samuel 15) relating how King David was abandoned and persecuted by his son and people; the crucifixion is prepared by a powerful scene (based on Judges 16) showing how Samson, by his great strength, brought destruction on the Philistines, losing his own life by the action; and, finally, the entombment and approaching resurrection of Christ is related to the scene of Jonah's shipwreck, preservation in the whale's belly and eventual restoration to dry land and life. Between each Old Testament scene and the succeeding portion of the Passion narrative there is a section of recitative and aria, marked *Die gläubige Anwendung* (the application to the Faith), in which the precise typological relationship is carefully spelt out and interpreted in detail so as to avoid any possible misunderstanding on the part of the congregation. During the later part of the Baroque period typology, as a system of biblical inter-

---

[1] The extent to which this typological relationship between Joseph and Christ was an accepted part of Lutheran theology is clearly and concisely demonstrated in the following verse by the sixteenth-century poet, Nikolaus Herman:

> 'Joseph ein rechtes Fürbild ist
> Unsers Heilandes Jesu Christ,
> Den Judas hat verraten
> Und verkauft in der Juden Hand,
> Da litt er Hohn, Spott, Schmach und Schand,
> Joseph war Christi Schatten.'

(From P. Wackernagel, *Das deutsche Kirchenlied von der ältesten Zeit bis zu Anfang des XVII. Jahrhunderts*, Vol. III, No. 1394.)

pretation, was an important feature of Lutheran theology and had a considerable influence on the construction of cantata texts, notably those set by J. S. Bach (see H. Werthemann, *Die Bedeutung der alttestamentlichen Historien in Johann Sebastian Bachs Kantaten*, J. C. B. Mohr [Paul Siebeck], Tübingen, 1960). It is, however, most unusual to find such precisely drawn typological parallels in a Passion composition. The compilation of the libretto was the work of Matthaeus Arnold Wilkens, a friend of Brockes and Hagedorn, who also wrote the libretti for Telemann's Passions of 1735 and 1738.

Apart from the five Old Testament scenes and a final chorus in the conventional lullaby style, the only additional meditative commentary in this St Luke Passion consists of eight congregational chorales, the last of which concludes the whole work after the *Schluss-chor*. The entire musical setting of the actual Gospel account is, in fact, remarkably straightforward, approximating in style to some of the later seventeenth-century Oratorio Passions, such as those of Sebastiani, Theile and Meder. The Evangelist and the minor characters sing a simple form of operatic recitative accompanied by *continuo* alone; there is virtually no use of *melisma*, but some discreet mood-painting is occasionally achieved by harmonic colour, such as the Neapolitan sixth which underlies the account of the 'bitter weeping' of Peter. The sayings of Christ are also frequently supported only by *continuo*, but at certain focal points, notably for the words instituting the Holy Communion, for the intense prayers during the Agony in the Garden and for two of the utterances from the Cross, a simple independent accompaniment for strings is added. The function of the orchestra during the narrative of the Passion is generally very restrained; even the *turba* choruses lack independent accompaniment, the strings simply doubling the four voice-parts of the choir. But for the Old Testament preparatory scenes a rather richer scheme of orchestration is adopted, an attempt being made to characterize the different moods by contrasts of key and by the predominant colour of solo woodwind instruments. The disposition of the keys and instruments in the five scenes is as follows: (i) G minor—solo oboe, (ii) G major—solo bassoon, (iii) C minor—solo oboe, (iv) F major—solo oboe, (v) C major/F major—solo flute. In the final chorus the solo flute is again used and the basic tonality of G reappears.

Despite the novelty of the Old Testament preparatory scenes a Passion without direct, operatic interpolations into the Gospel account may well have seemed somewhat conservative at Hamburg in 1728; it is therefore rather surprising to find that Telemann turned to this simple form again at an even later date, 1735. This later work, a setting of St Mark, contains seven poetic soliloquies (the texts by M. A. Wilkens) which once again are not integrated with the biblical narrative but are kept quite separate, recalling the placing of the *Intermedia* in Thomas Selle's St John Passion (1643). Elsewhere in Telemann's settings there is a marked tendency to intersperse the liturgical Passion with elements drawn from the popular 'Opera' Passions of the period. Allegorical figures, such as 'Courage', 'Devotion', 'Reason', 'Religion' and 'Zeal', are introduced to sing sections of free reflective commentary, frequently set in the *da capo* aria form; furthermore, in some places, parts of the actual biblical account are presented in colourful verse paraphrases, and freely devised dramatic utterances are added to interrupt the Gospel narrative.

At times Telemann also contravenes an apparently basic rule of construction, as found in the Bach Passions, by breaking down the clear dividing line between the *dramatis personae* authorized by the Gospel account, who sing only the biblical words, and the solo singers (allegorical persons and others), who present the reflective commentary-texts. Several instances can be found where the Gospel characters step out of their proper dramatic context and become commentators in their own right. Indeed, in both the St Matthew Passion (1730) and the St Mark Passion (1759), Jesus himself, in defiance of the accepted dramatic unities, unexpectedly joins the ranks of the commentators, combining with a soprano soloist (representing a Sinner) in reflective duets; in the St Matthew setting the duet occurs after the scene of Peter's denial, where Jesus, moved by the tears of the Sinner, promises forgiveness to all who are truly repentant, while in the St Mark Passion the equivalent duet passage is a meditation upon the mockery of Jesus by the soldiers after his condemnation by Pilate. One further, very striking, instance of the same device occurs in the St Matthew Passion (1730) where Judas, conscience-stricken after his betrayal of Jesus, launches into a vividly dramatic *arioso* passage, marked *furioso*, which starts '*Ach wehe, wehe mir, was hab' ich denn begangen*' (Ah! woe is me, what then

have I done), continuing later with the words *'Wohlan, so will
ich selbst mein strenger Henker sein'* (Well then, I will my own
harsh hangman be). It should however be noticed that, during
this soliloquy, Judas does not move outside the dramatic
framework to become a detached commentator, but remains
'in character', expressing his thoughts by means of a text
added directly to the Gospel account.

In addition to these occasional examples where the characters fulfil a dual, dramatic and meditative, function, there are
also some interesting places in the St Matthew Passion (1730)
where short melodic ideas, set to parts of the dramatic Gospel
narrative, are integrated into the music of the succeeding meditative commentary with the clear intention of achieving greater
unity. The idea appears to have originated with Handel who,
in his St John Passion, introduced part of the theme set to
Jesus's utterance, *'Es ist vollbracht'* (It is finished), into the
great bass aria, *O grosses Werk*, which immediately follows
on as commentary. This example from Handel almost certainly served as a model for Bach who used the same device
in precisely the same context in his St John Passion (No. 57
and No. 58). The Gospel contexts in which Telemann employs
such thematic transference are different, but it seems nevertheless very probable that he, too, was following Handel's example. One instance occurs during the Crucifixion scene
where a chromatic melodic phrase set to Jesus's cry, *'Eli, Eli,
lama asabthani'* (and the Evangelist's translation) is interwoven into the succeeding reflective bass aria, *Gott ruft selbst:
Mein Gott, mein Gott, warum hast Du mich verlassen, warum,
warum?* A second example, from the same Passion, occurs
during the trial scene before Pilate, where the chorus re-echo,
with great effect, the crowd's cry of *'Barabbam'* during the succeeding tenor aria; this aria, *So gehet es, keiner rufet Jesum
und alle schreien Barabbam*, tells how, then and now, nothing
has changed, the demand of the crowd is always for Barabbas
(symbolizing worldly things) rather than Jesus.

Choral interjections of this type are rather rare in Passion
music, the best-known examples being the three places
in the Bach Passions (St Matthew Nos. 1 and 70 and St John
No. 48) where the chorus utter questioning cries of 'Come
where?', 'Look where?', etc., against a solo vocal line or a
semichorus background. As we have seen earlier (p. 99) these
Bach examples were clearly modelled on the aria with chorus,

Eilt, ihr angefochten Seelen, from Handel's Brockes Passion of 1716, where such choral interpolations appear to have been first used. It is therefore interesting to note that in his St Matthew Passion (1730), during the soprano aria with chorus, *Frohlocket, hochbetrübte Seelen*, Telemann employs exactly the same device, with similar questioning cries, *'Wodurch?'*, *'Womit?'*, *'Was denn?'*; there can be no doubt that in this case also Telemann, like Bach, borrowed the idea from Handel.

A final word may be added about Telemann's chorale settings. These are usually harmonized very simply, without elaborate passing-note treatment, their main purpose being clearly to give the congregation a positive rôle in the enactment of the drama. Telemann does not normally use chorale melodies in more complex musical designs, for example as *cantus firmi* in fantasia-like movements or as choral backgrounds to solo recitatives and arias, in the manner favoured by Bach. There is, however, one exception to this which deserves special comment. In the St Mark Passion (1759), immediately following the scene of the death of Christ, there is a splendidly rhetorical aria for solo bass, marked *'Die Stimme Gottes'* (The voice of God), in which it is announced that Jesus, crowned with glory and praise, has atoned through his blood and may now rest. In the accompaniment to this aria the orchestra, high above the voice, plays the melody of the famous chorale, *Lobt Gott, ihr Christen allzugleich* (1560) by Nikolaus Herman. The effect is most striking and impressive, and typical of the sort of imaginative stroke of which Telemann, so often in these Passion settings, proves himself capable.

BIBLIOGRAPHY

Abbreviations

AfMW   Archiv für Musikwissenschaft
BJ   Bach-Jahrbuch
FMS   Festschrift Max Schneider
FS   Festschrift Schering
JP   Jahrbuch Peters
LJ   Luther Jahrbuch
ML   Music and Letters
MMR   Monthly Musical Record
MQ   Musical Quarterly
TVNM   Tijdschrift der Vereeniging voor Nederlandsche Muziekgeschiedenis

ABRAHAM, G. *Passion Music in the 15th and 16th centuries,* MMR 83 (1953), pp. 208, 235.
———. *Passion Music from Schütz to Bach,* MMR 84 (1954), pp. 115, 152, 175.
ADAMS, H. M. *Passion Music before 1724,* ML VII (1926), pp. 258-64.
ADRIO, A. *Die Matthaeus-Passion von J. G. Kühnhausen (um 1700),* FS, 1937.
BIRKE, J. *Eine unbekannte anonyme Matthaeuspassion aus der zweiten Hälfte des 17. Jahrhunderts,* AfMW XV (1958), pp. 162-86.
BLANKENBURG,W. *Zu den Johannes-Passionen von Ludwig Daser (1578) und Leonard Lechner (1593),* Festschrift für W. Vetter.
BUKOFZER, M. *Music in the Baroque Era,* New York, 1947.
———. *Studies in Medieval and Renaissance Music,* New York, 1950.
DAVID, H., & MENDEL, A. *The Bach Reader,* New York, 1945 (1966).
DÜRR. A. *Beobachtungen am Autograph der Matthäus-Passion,* BJ 50 (1963-64), pp. 47-52.
———. *Zu den verschollenen Passionen Bachs,* BJ 38 (1949-50), pp. 81-99.
EINSTEIN, A. *Heinrich Schütz,* Kassel, 1928.
EPSTEIN, P. *Ein unbekanntes Passionsoratorium von Christian Flor (1667),* BJ 27 (1930), pp. 65-99.
———. *Zur Geschichte der deutschen Choralpassion,* JP 36 (1929), p. 35.

Fischer, K. von. *Zur Geschichte der Passionskomposition des 16. Jahrhunderts in Italien*, AfMW 11 (1954), pp. 189-205.

Gerber, R. *Passionsrezitativ bei H. Schütz*, Gütersloh, 1929.

Heuss, A. *Die Matthaeus Passion*, Leipzig, 1909.

Hörner, H. G. Ph. *Telemanns Passionsmusiken, ein Beitrag zur Geschichte der Passionsmusik in Hamburg*, Borna-Lipsia, 1933.

Jacobs, A. (ed.). *Choral Music*, Harmondsworth, 1963.

Jeppesen, K. *A forgotten master of the early 16th century: Gaspar de Albertis*, MQ 44 (1958), pp. 311-28.

Kade, O. *Die ältere Passionskomposition bis zum Jahre 1631*, Gütersloh, 1893.

Lott, W. *Zur Geschichte der Passionskomposition von 1650 bis 1800*, AfMW III (1921), p. 285.

———. *Zur Geschichte der Passionsmusiken auf Danziger Boden*, AfMW VII (1925), pp. 297-328.

Moser, H. J. *Heinrich Schütz*, Kassel, 1936.

———. *Heinrich Schütz, His Life and Work*, trans. by C. F. Pfatteicher, St. Louis, Mo., 1959.

———. *Heinrich Schütz, a short account of his life and works*, trans. & ed. by D. McCulloch, London, 1967.

Parry, C. H. H. *Johann Sebastian Bach*, London, 1909 (1946).

Pirro, A. H. *Schütz* (*Les Maîtres de la Musique*), Paris, 1913 (1924).

Reese, G. *Music in the Middle Ages*, New York, 1940.

———. *Music in the Renaissance*, New York, 1954.

Richter, B. Fr. *Zur Geschichte der Passionsaufführungen in Leipzig*, BJ 8 (1911), pp. 50-59.

Robertson, P. *A Critical Survey of the Motet Passion*, MS dissertation, London, 1957.

Schering, A. *Zur Markus-Passion und zur 'vierten' Passion*, BJ 36 (1939), pp. 1-32.

Schmidt, G. *Grundsätzliche Bemerkungen zur Geschichte der Passionshistorie*, AfMW (1960), pp. 100-25.

Schmitz, A. *Italienische Quellen zur Figuralpassion des 16. Jahrhunderts*, FMS, Halle, 1935, p. 94.

———. *Zur motettischen Passion des 16. Jahrhunderts*, AfMW 16 (1959), pp. 232-45.

Schofield, B., & Bukofzer, M. *A Newly-Discovered 15th-Century Manuscript of the English Chapel Royal*, MQ 32 (1946), p. 509, and MQ 33 (1947), p. 38.

Schweitzer, A. *J. S. Bach*, 1905, Eng. trans. 1911 (1923), new ed. 1935. (Dover reprint, 1966)

Serauky, W. *Die 'Johannes-Passion' von Bach und ihr Vorbild*, BJ 41 (1954), pp. 29-39.

Smend, F. *Bachs Markus-Passion*, BJ 37 (1940-48), pp. 1-35.

———. *Bachs Matthaeus-Passion*, BJ 25 (1928), pp. 1-95.

———. *Die Johannes-Passion von Bach*, BJ 23 (1926), pp. 105-28.

SMIJERS, A. *De Matthaeus-Passie van Obrecht*, TVNM XIV (1935), p. 182.

SPITTA, F. *Die Passionen von Heinrich Schütz*, Leipzig, 1886.

SPITTA, P. J. S. *Bach*, Leipzig, 1873-80, Eng. trans. 1899. (Dover reprint, 1951)

TERRY, C. S. *Bach, The Passions: Bk. 1, 1723-25; Bk. 2, 1729-31*, London, 1926.

————. *The Spurious Bach 'Lukas Passion'*, ML XIV (1932), pp. 207-21.

WILSON, S. *The Recitatives of the St Matthew Passion*, ML XVI (1935), pp. 208-25.

WUSTMANN, R. *Matthäuspassion, erster Teil*, BJ 6 (1909), pp. 129-43.

YOUNG, K. *The Drama of the Medieval Church*, Oxford, 1933 (repr. 1967).

LIST OF PASSIONS AVAILABLE
IN MODERN EDITIONS

Abbreviations

BA	Bärenreiter-Ausgabe, Kassel and Basel.
BGA	Bach-Gesamtausgabe, J. S. Bachs Werke, Leipzig 1851-99.
BV	Barocco Verlag, Vaduz (Liechtenstein).
CM	Collegium Musicum, gen. ed. Leo Schrade, Yale University.
CW	Das Chorwerk, gen. ed. F. Blume, Möseler Verlag, Wolfenbüttel.
DDT	Denkmäler deutscher Tonkunst, 1892-1931.
Eu	Ernst Eulenberg, Ltd. miniature scores.
HDK	Handbuch der deutschen evangelischen Kirchenmusik, Göttingen.
HHA	Hallische Händel-Ausgabe, Bärenreiter, Kassel and Basel.
MAM	Musik älterer Meister, Graz.
MD	Musikalische Denkmäler, Mainz.
MSv	Musica Svecica, Stockholm.
Mus.Brit	Musica Britannica.
Nov	Novello and Co., Ltd., London.
OLSW	Orlando di Lasso, Sämtliche Werke, Bärenreiter, Kassel and Basel.
TCM	Tudor Church Music, edd. P. C. Buck, E. H. Fellowes, et al., 10 vols., 1922–29.
TMW	Georg Philipp Telemann, Musikalische Werke, Bärenreiter, Kassel and Basel.
VOO	Thomae Ludovici Victoria, Opera Omnia, ed. P. Pedrell, Lipsiae, 1908. Reprint, Gregg Press, Ridgewood, N.J., 1966.

ANON. (Swedish). *St John*, ed. L. Reimers, MSv, XVII, 1, Stockholm, 1962.
G. M. ASOLA. *St John*, ed. A. Schmitz, MD, Vol. I, Mainz, 1955, p. 107.
J. E. BACH. *Passion Oratorio*, ed. J. Kromolicki, DDT, Vol. 48.
J. S. BACH. *St John*, BGA, XII[1], 3. Vocal score (English) ed. Atkins, Nov, London, 1929.

173

J. S. Bach. *St Luke*, BGA, XLV². Vocal score (abridged and revised) ed. M. Diack, Paterson's, London.
——. *St Mark*, ed. D. Hellmann, Hänssler, Stuttgart, 1964.
——. *St Matthew*, BGA, IV, 1. Vocal score (English) ed. Elgar and Atkins, Nov, London, 1938.
A. Beber. *St Mark*, ed. S. Wallon, CW, No. 66.
S. Besler. *St Matthew*, HDK, I, 3 and 4, Göttingen, 1937.
J. von Burck. *St John*, ed. F. Jöde, Möseler, Wolfenbüttel, 1957, and Hänssler, Stuttgart, 1959.
W. Byrd. *St John*, TCM, Vol. 7, 1927.
R. Davy. *St Matthew*, ed. F. Ll. Harrison, Mus.Brit, Vol. 12, The Eton Choirbook, p. 112.
C. Demantius. *St John*, ed. F. Blume, CW, No. 27.
F. Funcke (attrib.). *St Matthew*, ed. J. Birke, CW, No. 78/79.
B. Gesius. *St Matthew*, ed. F. Commer, Musica Sacra, VI, Berlin, 1861.
G. F. Handel. *Brockes Passion*, ed. F. Schroeder, HHA, Series 1, Vol. 7.
——. *St John*, The Works of G. F. Handel, Part IX, Breitkopf & Härtel, Leipzig, 1860.
J. Herold. *St Matthew*, ed. H. J. Moser, MAM, Graz, 1955.
Jaquet of Mantua. *St John*, ed. A. Schmitz, MD, Vol. 1., Mainz, 1955, p. 95.
J. Kühnhausen. *St Matthew*, ed. A. Adrio, CW, No. 50.
O. Lassus. *Four Passions* (Matthew, Mark, Luke, John), ed. K. von Fischer, OLSW, new series, Vol. 2.
L. Lechner. *St John*, ed. K. Ameln, BA, No. 70.
T. Mancinus. *St Matthew*, ed. F. Schmidt, BA, No. 266.
J. Meiland. *St Mark*, HDK, I, 3 and 4, Göttingen, 1939.
G. Nasco (Maistre Jehan). *St Matthew*, ed. A. Schmitz, MD, Vol. 1, Mainz, 1955, p. 1.
J. Obrecht (Longaval). *St Matthew*, in O. Kade, *Die ältere Passionskomposition*, Gütersloh, 1893, p. 246.
A. Pfleger. *Seven Last Words*, ed. F. Stein, CW, No. 52.
B. Resinarius. *St John*, edd. F. Blume and F. Schultze, CW, No. 47.
C. de Rore. *St John*, ed. A. Schmitz, MD, Vol. 1, Mainz, 1955, p. 59.
A. Scandello. *St John*, HDK, I, 3 and 4, Göttingen, 1937; and in O. Kade, *Die ältere Passionskomposition*, Gütersloh, 1893, p. 306.
A. Scarlatti. *St John*, ed. E. Hanley, CM, No. 1.
C. Schultze. *St Luke*, ed. P. Epstein, Breslauer-Verlag, Berlin, 1930.
H. Schütz. *Seven Last Words*, ed. F. Stein, Eu, No. 977.
——. *Three Passions* (Matthew, Luke, John), ed. F. Stein, Eu, Nos. 976, 978, 979.
(All four Schütz works also available in the Neuausgabe, Sämtliche Werke, II, Bärenreiter, 1957)
J. Sebastiani. *St Matthew*, ed. F. Zelle, DDT, Vol. 17.
T. Selle. *St John*, ed. R. Gerber, CW, No. 26.

G. P. TELEMANN. *St Luke* (1728), edd. H. Hörner and M. Ruhnke, TMW, Vol. XV, 1964.
————. *St Matthew* (1730), ed. K. Redel, BV, 1964.
J. THEILE. *St Matthew*, ed. F. Zelle, DDT, Vol. 17.
T. L. DE VICTORIA. *St John*, ed. P. Pedrell, VOO, Vol. 5, p. 170.
————. *St Matthew*, ed. P. Pedrell, VOO, Vol. 5, p. 113.
M. VULPIUS. *St Matthew*, ed. K. Ziebler, BA, No. 695.
J. WALTER. *St Matthew*, in O. Kade, *Die ältere Passionskomposition*, Gütersloh, 1893, p. 274.

INDEX

A CATALOGUE OF SELECTED DOVER BOOKS
IN ALL FIELDS OF INTEREST

A CATALOGUE OF SELECTED DOVER BOOKS
IN ALL FIELDS OF INTEREST

WHAT IS SCIENCE?, *N. Campbell*
The role of experiment and measurement, the function of mathematics, the nature of scientific laws, the difference between laws and theories, the limitations of science, and many similarly provocative topics are treated clearly and without technicalities by an eminent scientist. "Still an excellent introduction to scientific philosophy," H. Margenau in *Physics Today*. "A first-rate primer . . . deserves a wide audience," *Scientific American*. 192pp. 5⅜ x 8.
60043-2 Paperbound $1.25

THE NATURE OF LIGHT AND COLOUR IN THE OPEN AIR, *M. Minnaert*
Why are shadows sometimes blue, sometimes green, or other colors depending on the light and surroundings? What causes mirages? Why do multiple suns and moons appear in the sky? Professor Minnaert explains these unusual phenomena and hundreds of others in simple, easy-to-understand terms based on optical laws and the properties of light and color. No mathematics is required but artists, scientists, students, and everyone fascinated by these "tricks" of nature will find thousands of useful and amazing pieces of information. Hundreds of observational experiments are suggested which require no special equipment. 200 illustrations; 42 photos. xvi + 362pp. 5⅜ x 8.
20196-1 Paperbound $2.00

THE STRANGE STORY OF THE QUANTUM, AN ACCOUNT FOR THE GENERAL READER OF THE GROWTH OF IDEAS UNDERLYING OUR PRESENT ATOMIC KNOWLEDGE, *B. Hoffmann*
Presents lucidly and expertly, with barest amount of mathematics, the problems and theories which led to modern quantum physics. Dr. Hoffmann begins with the closing years of the 19th century, when certain trifling discrepancies were noticed, and with illuminating analogies and examples takes you through the brilliant concepts of Planck, Einstein, Pauli, Broglie, Bohr, Schroedinger, Heisenberg, Dirac, Sommerfeld, Feynman, etc. This edition includes a new, long postscript carrying the story through 1958. "Of the books attempting an account of the history and contents of our modern atomic physics which have come to my attention, this is the best," H. Margenau, Yale University, in *American Journal of Physics*. 32 tables and line illustrations. Index. 275pp. 5⅜ x 8.
20518-5 Paperbound $2.00

GREAT IDEAS OF MODERN MATHEMATICS: THEIR NATURE AND USE, *Jagjit Singh*
Reader with only high school math will understand main mathematical ideas of modern physics, astronomy, genetics, psychology, evolution, etc. better than many who use them as tools, but comprehend little of their basic structure. Author uses his wide knowledge of non-mathematical fields in brilliant exposition of differential equations, matrices, group theory, logic, statistics, problems of mathematical foundations, imaginary numbers, vectors, etc. Original publication. 2 appendixes. 2 indexes. 65 ills. 322pp. 5⅜ x 8.
20587-8 Paperbound $2.25

APPLIED OPTICS AND OPTICAL DESIGN,
A. E. Conrady
With publication of vol. 2, standard work for designers in optics is now complete for first time. Only work of its kind in English; only detailed work for practical designer and self-taught. Requires, for bulk of work, no math above trig. Step-by-step exposition, from fundamental concepts of geometrical, physical optics, to systematic study, design, of almost all types of optical systems. Vol. 1: all ordinary ray-tracing methods; primary aberrations; necessary higher aberration for design of telescopes, low-power microscopes, photographic equipment. Vol. 2: (Completed from author's notes by R. Kingslake, Dir. Optical Design, Eastman Kodak.) Special attention to high-power microscope, anastigmatic photographic objectives. "An indispensable work," *J., Optical Soc. of Amer.* Index. Bibliography. 193 diagrams. 852pp. 6⅛ x 9¼.
60611-2, 60612-0 Two volume set, paperbound $8.00

MECHANICS OF THE GYROSCOPE, THE DYNAMICS OF ROTATION,
R. F. Deimel, Professor of Mechanical Engineering at Stevens Institute of Technology
Elementary general treatment of dynamics of rotation, with special application of gyroscopic phenomena. No knowledge of vectors needed. Velocity of a moving curve, acceleration to a point, general equations of motion, gyroscopic horizon, free gyro, motion of discs, the damped gyro, 103 similar topics. Exercises. 75 figures. 208pp. 5⅜ x 8.
60066-1 Paperbound $1.75

STRENGTH OF MATERIALS,
J. P. Den Hartog
Full, clear treatment of elementary material (tension, torsion, bending, compound stresses, deflection of beams, etc.), plus much advanced material on engineering methods of great practical value: full treatment of the Mohr circle, lucid elementary discussions of the theory of the center of shear and the "Myosotis" method of calculating beam deflections, reinforced concrete, plastic deformations, photoelasticity, etc. In all sections, both general principles and concrete applications are given. Index. 186 figures (160 others in problem section). 350 problems, all with answers. List of formulas. viii + 323pp. 5⅜ x 8.
60755-0 Paperbound $2.50

HYDRAULIC TRANSIENTS,
G. R. Rich
The best text in hydraulics ever printed in English . . . by former Chief Design Engineer for T.V.A. Provides a transition from the basic differential equations of hydraulic transient theory to the arithmetic integration computation required by practicing engineers. Sections cover Water Hammer, Turbine Speed Regulation, Stability of Governing, Water-Hammer Pressures in Pump Discharge Lines, The Differential and Restricted Orifice Surge Tanks, The Normalized Surge Tank Charts of Calame and Gaden, Navigation Locks, Surges in Power Canals—Tidal Harmonics, etc. Revised and enlarged. Author's prefaces. Index. xiv + 409pp. 5⅜ x 8½.
60116-1 Paperbound $2.50